Lemons into Lemonade
without the SUGAR

Lemons into Lemonade without the SUGAR

✦

Includes "Time Life LOVE TIME ORIGINAL FORMULA"

Written by Ana H. B. Weber

Clock and hat designs by Storm Design England

iUniverse, Inc.
New York Lincoln Shanghai

Lemons into Lemonade without the SUGAR
Includes "Time Life LOVE TIME ORIGINAL FORMULA"

iUniverse books may be ordered through booksellers or by contacting:

iUniverse
2021 Pine Lake Road, Suite 100
Lincoln, NE 68512
www.iuniverse.com
1-800-Authors (1-800-288-4677)

ISBN-13: 978-0-595-41300-3 (pbk)
ISBN-13: 978-0-595-85655-8 (ebk)
ISBN-10: 0-595-41300-5 (pbk)
ISBN-10: 0-595-85655-1 (ebk)

Printed in the United States of America

I DEDICATE THIS BOOK WITH ALL MY
LOVE AND JOY TO:

My Mother Erzsebeth for her 90th birthday,
to my ONLY son Sean,
my daughter in law Sarah and
to my grandchildren LOGAN AND MIA.
You are my shinning stars.

Contents

Introduction

Glancing at the title on the cover, you probably wondered, What is this book all about? Is it a recipe of some sort? Or does it deliver an entirely different message?

This book has two parts. In the first, I share with you my personal life as a child and the challenges and obstacles I had to overcome. I also explore how circumstances dictate personality—specifically, why and in what manner an isolated individual, shy and lacking confidence, can turn around completely. It also teaches the value of relationships, including their impact and the vital necessity of building relationships. I believe that the trick is to learn how to maintain our relationships, as well as the manner we choose to bring closure to a relationship when the situation requires us to do so.

In the second part, I introduce you to one of the most important of all relationships: the one we have with *time*. How can we develop a beneficial, intimate relationship with time? How can we acknowledge time, be grateful for it, accomplish more with it and enjoy the time between destinations as we reach our goals?

Ask yourself these questions: Where would we be without time? What could we accomplish and enjoy without time? Do we utilize time correctly and wisely?

The answers I provide are simple, clear and useful.

Extract your own ideas and wisdom from this book. Be patient and listen to the sound of the words and the feelings involved, and without any effort you will be drawn into the picture very easily. Make yourself comfortable wherever you choose; sit down and let go of all distractions.

Stay with me.

I am quite certain that you have heard the expression "turning lemons into lemonade," or something close to those words with the same intention.

The meaning remains the same, just painted in a different color. To make the statement in a more powerful way and with additional strength and depth, I have decided to add the words "without the sugar" so you can be touched in a sincere, genuine way as I gently awaken your feelings about the reality that only you can live. For me, this approach has made all the difference, and I passionately believe that with an inquisitive mind you will understand the message.

Most of us enjoy a cold, fresh drink of lemonade, especially on a hot summer day. But without the sugar? Is that possible? How is it done? And how did the people in this book do it? It was a matter of choice, of detaching logic from emotions, using common sense and letting the ego go elsewhere. You may also need to put forth the effort to feel the outcome of future events in advance.

In figurative speech, the word *lemon* tends to magnify the sourness of an object or situation. It represents a distastefulness that did not agree with us, or the fact that we purchased a physical object that did not work or perform according to our expectations. How many times have you heard someone say, "My car was a lemon, so I had to return it to the dealer"?

The impact of my personal story, and the events that other individuals shared firsthand, led me to the present moment. I had to release them all to you. You may feel that the life you live is more difficult, even completely unbearable. You are not alone! We are all given our share of challenges to deal with. This is the one and only thing we have in common. But we are free to choose our approach, our determination and our feelings in dealing with the obstacles that hit us one after another.

The best education one can receive, in referring to relationships and the challenges of life in general, comes from looking at them and accepting them as real experiences, true stories and incredible triumphs, regardless of the adversities and seemingly impossible situations in which we find ourselves. We use approximately 5 to 8 percent of our brainpower during our lives. Can you imagine how much more we could achieve if we take it a bit further?

We can!

My intention is to enlighten you and share how I overcame the challenges I faced. They were never easy. Like you, I wondered, *Why me? Why do I have to go through this? Why can't I have what others have? Why does everything in life come to me with such difficulty? Why do others have it so easy? Why can't I be more successful? Why am I wrapped up with all this negativity? Why is my health troubled? Why can't I be more attractive? Why is school so hard for me? Why are there so many obstacles in life? Why am I not loved? Why am I always living paycheck to paycheck? Why do I never seem to have enough to do the extra things I dream about, such as visiting far-away countries? Why is my life so uneventful and boring? Why do I hate my job so much?* These and all the other whys continue as time moves forward.

I've been there!

It is now my great pleasure to validate your feelings and emotions.

The big question, I've come to realize, is "Why?" What do I mean by that? Our personal why holds the hidden secret to everything, and when we arrive at that station in our lives, all the hows will come one by one. Our understanding of all that reality dishes out to us will unfold the mysteries of the dark moments, the unpleasant events, the disappointments and hardships that we find so heavy and that drag us down with such force. One can choose to live life fully. This is not unattainable. One can get there. I did. I am so thrilled to invite you into my personal story, my triumphs, and the feelings I have for every one of you.

No one ever promised us that we would be beautiful, skinny, kind, loving, happy and exciting all at the same time. It's not supposed to be that way. The imperfections in our lives and the uniqueness we possess are the keys to our contentment and fulfillment. The balance we achieve through our journey and the colors painted from within can be embraced with humility, love, appreciation and exuberance.

Life is everything, and the seed that grows with time needs replanting, refurbishing and lots of care. Let us not neglect it. After all, what is everything else without it? Absolutely nothing.

Earlier, when I mentioned the personal why, this is what I meant. We cannot live anyone else's life but our own. That is why it is so special. When we are centered and understand our why as our personal path, one that has a "Do Not Enter" sign, that is when we can enjoy every moment of our lives and be enthused about our passions, our goals, our accomplishments, our progress and our outlook toward everyone and everything outside our personal circle of life.

That does not mean we should be self-centered and never think of anyone else. On the contrary, when we make others more important, validate their feelings and make ourselves available for them, that is when our energies become a fascinating tool for our own happiness. When we devote most of our time to our egos and our materialistic desires, and when we compete with others thinking that we can do better, look better or have more financial freedom, regardless of the price we have to pay—that is when we become too absorbed and clutter overwhelms us. That is when we experience health issues, weight fluctuations and acceleration of the aging process. We look and feel miserable about everyone and everything. Most importantly, our energies are uncontrollably diverted toward those negative feelings and emotions. The drive becomes harder, the hills get higher and higher, and as we keep raising the speed limit the challenge meets us head-on. The mountains appear ahead of us over and over again. There is a chill in our spine and we seem lost and bothered. At such times we choose to feel less, thinking that might work. But to our amazement it does not.

What a pity. When people choose to walk their own exclusive paths, manage their lives and keep pace with their abilities and desires, they make it over those hills and mountains with less effort. Their energies are not depleted and their clarity of mind shows simpler solutions with fewer challenges.

This alternative is much more fulfilling. And we always have the opportunity to choose it.

When we figure out our personal whys and follow our own passions and not those of others, developing our talents and special skills, we grow. We not only become less dependent on other people's feelings for support, we also become focused and much more fulfilled. Remember, everyone is good at something. Everyone is special in his or her own way. Everyone can be happy. Everyone is unique and imperfect, regardless of all the makeovers available. The most valuable makeover is the one built from within. You will have that one for your entire lifetime, and you will never need to redo or enhance it. It will keep you company wherever you go and whatever you do. When you ask yourself, "Why do I want to go to school?" you will know the answer, just as when you ask, "Why do I seek this knowledge? Why does it mean so much to me? Why do I love this person so much? Why do I want to go there?" And so on and so on.

Now please do not misunderstand me. One can pursue an exterior makeover only to fit their inner being. When one follows the dream of looking perfect from the outside, one achieves temporary satisfaction and admiration. But such things do not last, and the momentary praise will not keep you strong and together when challenges rock your life. Eventually you will need help, and in time everything that was renewed from the outside will fade away.

Instead, we must grow from within and keep our attitudes young toward the experience of simply living. Yes, we should not neglect to take care of ourselves with healthy diets, exercise and releasing stress. Enjoying better clothes, a newer vehicle to drive, frequent vacations, lovelier homes and entertainment are important. But we must be careful not to fall off the track. Think of your why and design and build from within at all times during your journey.

I am doing it, and so can you.

Enjoy the personal stories and tips in this book. You will be amazed at how these simple, practical ideas fit into your life, too, as long as you understand that the feelings will always be there and that life is empty without them. The facts and reality will enter your space anyway, whether invited or not, but you must make time to deal with them.

Time is the magnificent tool providing you with results. It stops for no one. Did you ever say to yourself, *I wish I could buy more time to do this or that? I need more time to accomplish certain tasks. If only I could turn back time! If only tomorrow would come sooner! Why is time moving so quickly?* Sometimes we would LOVE to stop time from going forward at such a furious pace.

Funny, isn't it? Actually, time is the most serious and treasured tool we have. Time is our best friend, the one we should love with all our hearts. It moves on without stopping, brings in the new and washes out the old and embattled past.

I love time. I treat it with kindness and, most importantly, with value. I relate to time. Through my personal experiences and challenges, I have developed an incredibly intimate relationship with time.

And so can you.

Life is colorful, designed for each and every one of us in different shapes. It is supposed to be that way. When one tries to take on someone else's life, one soon realizes that it does not fit. The choice will only cause turmoil, anxiety and unfamiliarity. Why? Simply because it is not yours. When we understand and grasp this simple common-sense concept, we become free, and all the negativity that previously occupied our lives vanishes. When we have clean space in our hearts and our minds, the new and the fresh enters. Isn't that wonderful? *Change* is a special friend you can actually walk with. One cannot walk away from change. It's the wind in our sails.

Can you imagine remaining a baby forever and never talking, walking or growing? What if you never knew anything but that very first hour of your life? We are all born only as receivers. As we grow, we must learn and practice the art of giving and yet still hold onto the importance of taking care of ourselves. The best giver is a good taker. This is a valuable balance we need to understand and apply.

Now you see what I mean about the seed of life. The seed grows and flowers, and with time it will perform anything and everything we desire, as long as we understand that change. Such change is inevitable, and we can always choose with both feelings and logic, taking into consideration our real world and selecting the ones that belong only to us.

Celebrate life from the inside out. Have a wonderful journey. We can always use our feelings, our logic and our understanding of the real world to choose which changes belong to us and no one else.

Ana H.B. Weber

PART I

1

The chilly, stormy, unwelcome weather came early to my home city of Cluj, Romania, that winter. It was early December, but usually the heavy snows and strong winds came in January. This year, however, everything seemed different, and the scenery turned gray and somber.

Three months before, I had turned seven years old. As I stood in line with my mother, waiting to purchase a loaf of bread, a hot sweat overtook my entire body. It felt like a volcano had erupted within me, and the heat flushing through my veins did not feel right. At first I did not know what to do or say, and the unexpected feeling became stronger and harder to bear. I was a very thin, pale little girl and I felt that I was already grown up. I definitely did not feel like a child. Life and circumstances had catapulted me into adulthood.

You see, I am an only child, and my parents got divorced when I was five years old. I lived with Mom, and Dad would visit me once a week. We never got very close. All I knew was that he was my dad and that was it. They both claimed that they had different outlooks on and expectations from life. They had to follow their own dreams.

Today I understand this better than ever. Life has taught me tremendous lessons.

Times were difficult and not terribly free or open then. I was a very shy, insecure little girl. I was taught by my mother not to speak unless I was asked a question and not to volunteer any information unless it was related to school or academic material

I had learned. I chose to stay quietly in my own little sheltered world. It felt safe and untroubled.

Our apartment was on the third floor of an old building—45 steps and a beat-up elevator with black steel doors that did not work. At any rate, it was good exercise. The only time that I felt out of breath was when my stomach was empty and I had to carry a briefcase full of books and notebooks, as well as a few groceries in a sheer, colorful, knitted nylon satchel. We had no grocery bags or paper bags at the time. I was a good runner, and gymnastics was an important part of our education, so the stairs were not much of a task for me.

My briefcase was heavy even without the contents, so you can imagine that with everything it weighed approximately 15 pounds, and I only weighed 55 pounds, if memory serves and I have correctly converted my weight from kilograms.

Our house was in a good neighborhood in Romania, located several blocks from the university grounds where thousands of people would come to visit and admire the famous botanical gardens.

It was designed beautifully and the colorful flowers and plants were a magical sight. We would visit there, too, at least a couple of times a year. I can say that not many little children lived in the area where I grew up. It was more of an adult neighborhood, and at the age of seven I fit in perfectly.

We lived in a large studio apartment with a wide window. It was all we could afford in those times and that was all we knew, a reality we had to accept.

We shared the bathroom with two other families, and my bath turns were Tuesday and Friday. I cannot tell you how much I looked forward to those days. The rest of the week I used the kitchen sink to wash my young, thin body. It was not actually a separate kitchen. It was a sink, a counter and a stove built to the left of our living room. On the opposite side of the room was our bedroom, an incredible wooden bed set, a large bed, one nightstand, a dresser with a three-sided mirror, drawers and two brass lights in the shape of a snake. It is funny how one can go back so many years and remember such a detail as the snake lights. Somehow it will always stay with me.

A successful doctor who committed suicide a few years earlier had owned the furniture. He performed surgery on a young lady, and she died on the operating table. He was a fine man, but the guilt overtook him with such power that he no longer wished to live. My father knew of him, and due to the fact that the doctor had no family, my dad was able to purchase the furniture from the government. Perhaps I remember the details of the furniture so well because it was so beautifully crafted. Even though I've traveled quite a bit and have visited many exclusive antique and furniture stores, I have never seen another piece like it. We had to give our furniture back to the government, and the day we left the country I quietly waved good-bye to my special mirrored dresser set and the snake lights that looked down at me. I thought they could speak, too.

So let's go back to the moment when I stood in line with my mother, patiently waiting to purchase the special bread we loved so. It had a dark brown crust, and the inside of it tasted sweet and fluffy. My favorite thing was to take two slices of the bread, spread homemade butter that we had purchased from the local gypsies, and add to it slices of red or green peppers, if they were available at the open market stands. I liked it with sliced radishes, too, or the homemade jam my mother made occasionally. It was a treat for me, and I used to hide the bread under my coat when the weather was cold outside, because I preferred to eat it warm and fresh. This might sound absurd or unreal to you, but believe me, this was the life I knew at that age. Would I be the person I am today if not for those experiences? Absolutely not!

That early morning was the first day of winter vacation; kids did not go to school and many adults did not work, either. They had to clear the heavy snowfall from the paths, and the roads were completely blocked. Therefore the lines for the bread were incredibly long, and the breath from people's mouths formed an additional line of white smoke standing out so clearly in the chilly air.

By the time our turn came to buy bread, my legs had grown weak, and I had to hold onto the counter with my icy, wool-gloved hands to keep from falling down. The next thing I remember is my mother asking me with concern, "Why is your face so red?" When she touched my cheeks, she instantly knew the answer. "You must have a very high fever. Let's go home quickly."

She took me by the arm while holding the bread underneath her coat with her other hand. I did not feel my steps. It seemed to me that I was flying, and the distance back home was endless and cruel. The moment we entered our apartment, I fell down on my bed and passed out.

An epidemic of scarlet fever had hit the town earlier that week, and kids between the ages of six and twelve came down with the illness. Some of them stayed home with doctors' visitations. Others had it so badly that they had to go to the children's hospital, located a great distance from my home.

I was among the worst cases. As soon as the doctor came to visit, he told my mother clearly and sharply, "Your daughter is very ill. She must go to the hospital immediately. As a matter of fact, her situation is so bad that she cannot share a room with others. She must be isolated. No one will be able to visit her. She is too contagious and very far advanced."

My mother started to sob. "I can't believe this. She is too little to be by herself."

The doctor remained firm. "Your daughter can look outside her hospital room window and wave to you, but that's it. You can see her from the pavement below."

My mother's body began to shake and she continued to cry uncontrollably. "This cannot happen to us," she said weakly. "My little girl is all I have, and I don't know how to deal with this!"

"You must," the doctor said. "You want her to live, don't you?"

"Yes, yes!" my mother cried out.

The doctor called for a cab, and within 25 minutes we arrived at the hospital. His diagnosis was confirmed immediately. My mother would have to let me go if she chose life for me; it was as simple as that. She was not even permitted to hug me or give me a kiss. She waved to me with the saddest eyes I could ever remember, and I felt her pain. She packed a few little items for me in a bag: some homemade cookies, an apple, a book with lots of colorful illustrations and my one-inch wooden doll. I named her Rozsika. That is the only item I still have, along with the memories that take me back to that terrible day, a reality too cruel to deal with at such an early age.

The nurse, wearing a white mask on her face, took me up to the third floor of the building, then to a very small room. Luckily the room did have a large window looking outside. There was a small bed completely covered with a gray-and-red-striped wool blanket that seemed too rough even to the eye, one narrow pillow, and white steel rails with the color fading on the lower parts. A purple two-drawer nightstand was positioned to the right of the bed.

It looked old and worn, but it had a purpose. I got undressed and put on red flannel pajamas provided by the hospital. As soon as I put on the pajamas I felt even warmer than before. The nurse helped me take off my coat, my gloves, the thick brown turtleneck sweater, my brown wool pants, the rubber-soled boots and my wool socks, then placed them in the night-stand drawers.

A little square table covered with a white tablecloth and a wooden chair stood next to the nightstand. The room looked cold and terribly isolated, and I felt just the same: alone, sick, burning with fever, weak and cut off from my mother and the life I knew outside those walls. I had no energy to walk over to the window, but I knew that she was standing there outside, hoping for a glimpse of me. I fell asleep that afternoon without dinner or a cup of warm milk.

I woke up the next morning and my surroundings seemed so foreign and unpleasant. But I knew at once that I was ill and had to be there in order to get well. I hoped I would get out soon.

They served me breakfast, a cup of tea with a bit of sugar and one cold slice of bread with jam. I could barely eat, but I knew that I must. I stared at the pills on a small plate on the tray.

The nurse did not ask me how I felt or how I had slept. All she said was, "You must finish your bread and your tea and take those pills immediately after. If not, you will never get better."

I listened and, with a sharp, sour throat and pain all over my body, I ate the slice of bread, drank my tea and took the pills as quickly as I could swallow them.

The nurse walked out of the room. Only when she closed the heavy door behind her did I understand completely that I was locked in. I heard the unkind sound of the key turning in the knob, and as I looked more carefully I noticed that the door had a large black metal handle and a big keyhole. I was locked in, without a radio, without anybody's kind words or a song or even a sweet hello. All I could hear was the rapid beating of my heart, and I spoke to it softly. "I have to be strong," I said, "and my health will improve." I had no choice but to believe this. And with a last bit of strength, I got out of my bed and walked over to the window.

I was not surprised at what I saw. I knew deep in my entire being that Mom would be standing there, waiting to see my face from far away. And indeed there she was, waving to me with a smile. I waved back to her with a forced smile of my own. I was sad and my head felt almost detached from my body, but nevertheless I smiled. I knew she would feel much more at ease if I did that. As she walked away, she gave me a sign that she would be back soon. And I knew she would.

Mother had to run a small kiosk in the middle of town. My dad got her the job right after their divorce. The kiosk sold cigars, handmade rolled cigarettes, stationery, postcards, stamps, newspapers and magazines. Business was good and Mom ran it in twelve-hour shifts every other day. She had a lady partner who worked the days she was off. The kiosk had a great location, right next to a residential area as well as some offices and the Russian consulate. The best customers came from the consulate, and my very favorite was Mr. Smitku. Every time he made a purchase he brought me Russian chocolates wrapped in gold foil. How I loved those chocolates. I made flower shapes and butterflies out of the foil. Mr. Smitku had a way with kids; he had two of his own and missed seeing them when he was away. I also learned how to roll the tobacco in the fine, greasy paper and organize the stationery shelves for my mother.

I loved to keep busy after my homework was done. On the days my mother worked, I walked there after school. We ate leftovers heated on an old-fashioned oil-fired heater. As soon as I finished my home studies, I watched the people walking by while I did something with my hands, like rolling the tobacco, writing down the feelings I had that day or the events that had happened at school, and organizing the stationery on the shelves.

On the days Mother did not work, we went to the open market to buy some of the in-season produce. Mother and I frequently visited the movie theater to watch foreign films, especially ones from India. Those were emotional life stories with so much drama. At least once a month we went to the opera, the ballet, a classical concert or the theater. I cannot say that I did not receive a cultural education from an early age, even though our life was rough and tough. Culture was a big part of the lifestyle there, and most of the time we got free tickets for the events; my dad was involved in charity groups and he brought them to us. He knew how important it was for us to get out and have fun.

Once in a while, when Mom did not feel like cooking, we would go to the cantina and eat with the local workers. It was okay; usually they served some type of goulash with potatoes and peasant bread.

For birthdays and special occasions, Mom would take me to one of the finer restaurants a few blocks from home, and I would order my favorite meal: roasted veal with mashed potatoes, green peas, and a baked apple for dessert.

I felt really lucky whenever Mother purchased an orange for me. They were imported from Italy or Spain, and as soon as I entered our apartment the delightful scent of the orange would greet me.

I always peeled it carefully, so as not to waste any of it, and then shared it with my mom. Most of the time she took only a slice. I knew that all she wanted was to make me happy and give me the feeling that I had it all and lacked nothing. I had very few pieces of clothing, but they were well-made and custom-tailored by my father's friend. My dad was a top clothing designer who had studied in Switzerland, but his expertise was for men only.

Mom always bought me beautiful shoes. I remember my very special first pair of boots. I loved them so. They were gray leather and matched my gray wool coat. When I went out wearing the coat and the boots, I felt important and happy. I knew how to appreciate it all. Ours was not a life of quantity. I had very few material things, but I learned even then that quality makes a difference.

On the days Mother worked, she left the house very early. She would go to the warehouse at six a.m. and fill up her inventory. I, on the other hand, would get up at seven a.m., dress, and walk one block down to the local bakery and coffee shop. Mom introduced me to the workers, and I ate my breakfast there before walking on to school. They served me a fresh horn with butter and a large cup of hot chocolate. My table next to the window was always waiting for me, and the workers from the neighborhood never took a seat there. They were regular customers, and in time they got to know the days I came in. I was the only little girl there eating breakfast all by herself. We didn't need to speak to each other; we said it all with our expressions. We greeted each other with nods of our heads, that was all. And when I finished my horn and the hot chocolate, I had new energy to walk the additional three miles to school. It felt good.

During the summer, Mother took an entire month of vacation. As was the custom, we took the train or the bus to the mountains. There was a place called Borsec, at an elevation of about 10,000 feet. Borsec was a small town with many bed-and-breakfast *pensions* peeking through the lush pine trees. The roads were not paved, not even the main one. You could spot cows on the streets, walking back home in the late afternoon. The village had an open outdoor market with lots of fresh produce, a meat market and a fishpond.

But most vividly I remember the numerous caves within the mountains. Even in the month of August, you could walk in and various artistically-shaped ice stalactites hanging from the top would greet you, along with the darkness and the cold temperature. Borsec is also famous for its sparkling mineral waters pouring out of the mountains, so easy to reach and so refreshing to drink. Each and every water fountain had a specific healing purpose. They were designated for such illnesses as stomach problems, heart conditions, blood pressure, digestion, skin and so forth. I used to go to the mountains and carry a big jug with me so I could fill it up for the day. Unlike back home, I was never thirsty there. I never drank so much water. It did not taste the same, and I loved the bubbles in it.

2

I still do not know why, but after being in the hospital for two weeks my situation got worse. The doctor did not clearly explain to me why. Perhaps he did not know the reason himself. All I remember is that he informed me I would have to stay there for the entire month of December, and perhaps January as well.

Mother's face through the foggy window looked sadder to me every day. The expression of anxiety was written all over her features, and I had no answers. She would bring cigarettes and candy for the nursing staff, and they allowed her to send a few goodies up to me, like roasted chestnuts and my favorite treat, the chocolates that Mr. Smitku brought from the Russian consulate; books to read; some sharpened pencils; and a thick notebook. I wanted to write, and she knew how valuable those last few items were for releasing and expressing my feelings of isolation and despair.

Dad would come to see me, too, and once in a while he would send up some hot, freshly-roasted chestnuts and a hard candy for me.

My very best day in the hospital was when the nurse opened the door and I spotted an old, beat-up radio in her hands.

"Your dad sent it up to you, so you could listen to music and hear people talking."

Tears rolled uncontrollably down my hot face. How I missed voices, singing, the presence of people in my life. I had a friend that day, and I took the radio into my two hands and hugged it as if it were the most precious treasure ever given to me. My world felt less lonely. But as the month of January began, I grew less hopeful and more anxious to go home.

In the third week of January, Mother almost collapsed emotionally, and for once in their lives my parents agreed on the same plan. They had to take me out of the hospital and bring me home. They knew it could be life-threatening, but they chose that course. They bribed the nurses and guards with lots of goodies that were unavailable in the marketplace, plus some cash. Late one afternoon, just before the shift change to the night crew, they sent a couple of nurses up to my room. They dressed me quickly and bundled me in two thick blankets. I could hardly breathe.

The elderly nurse whispered to me, "Don't be alarmed. Your mother is taking you home. She is downstairs waiting for you with a car and a home nurse, and your dad, as well."

I said nothing in return. All I could focus on was the happy beating of my heart and the easing of my mind. *No more isolation for me,* I thought. *Finally I am free.*

How little I knew then.

I was placed in the car, feeling very much like packaged goods. Within half an hour I was lying in my own bed. For a while the familiar surroundings lifted me from my torpor. But by week's end my illness had worsened and the doctor had to come daily to inject me with antibiotics. I had three rough weeks at home—coughing, high fever, weight loss and weakness. The illness took away any desire to eat or even listen to the radio. I did not have the strength to write one simple word in my notepad.

I remember very clearly my mother's face wrapped in such deep concern and guilt. She was searching for a miracle.

And then something incredible happened. It was January 30th, and when I woke up a clear blue sky greeted me through the window. A bright orange sun shone into our room. I got out of bed and went over to the sink to wash my face and hands. Mother was leaning against the stove, cooking some eggs and fresh chicken soup with lots of vegetables. That was considered a luxury. She looked at me with sad eyes and asked me to go back to bed.

I answered her with a stronger voice than the day before. "No, Mom. Please pull a chair up next to the window. I want to look outside and feel the heat of the sun on my body."

"Are you really up to it?"

"Yes," I said with a smile.

She pulled the chair up next to the window and sat down comfortably. The sun hugged me with such love. Mom made me breakfast. She put a soft-boiled egg and a slice of bread on a silver tray and I started to eat. A baby bluebird landed on our windowsill, and I felt such a connection with the bird. It brought an unspoken message: *Your illness is beginning to drift away*. At least that is what I felt. And so it was.

That sunny day in January, after two months of scarlet fever, was the beginning of the healing period. I felt even better the next day. By the second week I was able to go outside. In February I had my very first day back at school. The kids were surprised to see me, but they seemed pleased, and the teachers welcomed me. When I walked home from school, Mother had to carry most of my books and assignments. I had missed two months, so I had to catch up on lots of material.

And I did.

It was the continuation of my old life. Scarlet fever was a terrible memory from the past. But the isolation and the closed-off, lonely life would rock my world all over again a year later. How little we know about the future and the destiny that we do not have the ability to change, at least not when we are so young and vulnerable, facing the world and the consequences of other people's choices.

3

It was a hot summer day in August. School was out and I remained busy with reading, painting and keeping myself occupied at the cigarette and stationery kiosk on the days Mom worked a full twelve-hour shift. But that particular day was special for me. The neighbors across from the kiosk had a little girl almost my age, and I was allowed to play with her and her dollhouses for the whole afternoon. We had known the family for quite some time, and for a change Mom felt comfortable letting me go there.

We played for a couple of hours, and the hot summer wind was blowing gently through the small window in her bedroom. The white lace curtains fluttered back and forth, following the beat of the wind.

As the daylight began to fade with the setting sun, we got hungry and tired. I asked my friend, whose name was Monica, if we could go downstairs to my mom's place and get something to eat. Mom always had something stashed away, an apple, homemade butter cookies or just a few slices of bread and jam. I was ready to eat anything by that time. Monica was eager to join me.

As we opened her old wooden door, Monica's two brothers were there, standing between her dad and us. At first they smiled, asking us where we were headed in such a hurry, but at the same time they blocked the exit.

We said very softly that we were going down to the kiosk to get something to eat. Her mother had gone shopping and her grandma was sleeping in the back room.

"No, don't do that," her brother said. "We have plenty to eat. As a matter of fact, why don't we go for a bite at the local pub? It's just around the block. Don't you want a piece of fried chicken?" he added with a funny look on his face.

It sounded great, and like magnets we followed her father and two brothers out of the building. We walked straight down the street without even looking at my mom's kiosk.

We never made it to the pub.

As soon as we got to the corner of the street, her brother grabbed my arm firmly and asked me to hurry up. Monica's father grabbed her arm and we began to walk faster and faster, doing as we were told. I was so naive and sheltered, not street-smart, but with a sickening feeling in my stomach I knew that something was very wrong.

As we walked quickly to the end of the narrow street, her father opened the doors to an old station wagon. We were asked to get in. I knew at that very moment that I had better follow orders, so I stayed with Monica. I did not look at anyone. I said and asked nothing, and my stomach felt emptier and emptier as we drove away along the gray, deserted city streets.

We arrived at an open area. It was pitch-dark by then. We were told to get out of the car, and we did so without a word. The three men asked us to follow them and we did. I remember looking down and walking as quickly as I could. Within min-utes we were in a lush, rich forest, the one adjacent to the city river. I had gone there once before with some friends of my par-ents, fishing and walking close to the water, searching for tiny pebbles, but that was during the day. This time everything seemed too quiet, too peaceful, and yet my heart was bouncing up and down as if it wanted to jump into the water.

We were led to an old house, more like a shack, and ushered in without a word. The father lit a few candles, and with a little bit of light I could see that the room was completely empty except for a pair of chairs, a bottle of water and a few apples on a piece of wooden furniture. How I wished to have one of the apples, but I did not dare to ask. And then, as the light flickered over their faces, I understood that they did not have good thoughts in their minds.

But what about Monica? I thought. *They wouldn't hurt her.*

All of a sudden Monica's younger brother entered the room, pulled her by the arm and took her outside. I heard the car engine starting, and only then did I know that I was all alone in the dark with three strange men. I did not cry; I did not make a sound. I took it all in, and even today I can remember the chill running up and down my spine, the weakness in my legs and my empty stomach rumbling so loud that I could not hide it. They were up to no good. I had been kidnapped.

At the same time my mom was running through the streets of the city in a panic, trying to figure out where we were. What had happened to us? She was practically out of her mind.

She looked for my dad, who lived on the other side of town. As soon as he heard the news he ran with her directly to the police station. Thank God he had friends there. The Chief of Police and some of the judges were his clients. Several policemen left the precinct with four German shepherd dogs and started searching. Apparently one of the detectives suspected that something bad had happened. The dogs led them to the forest and by 10 p.m. I was saved.

When I saw my mom and dad, I could not say a word. All I remember is that she held me so tightly I could hardly breathe. I will never forget her cry. It was the most painful I have ever heard. Dad looked as pale as the first winter snow.

Needless to say, my life became even more isolated and protected after that incident. I was never again allowed to walk to school alone. I could not play with anyone. Fear ran our lives. My childhood seemed to be in the distant past. I felt so grown-up and serious. Play without worry was no longer a familiar notion to me. Now I had to face my feelings and my life.

4

The next few years were pretty uneventful. I went to school and tried very hard to be a good student. Gymnastics and music were the best parts of my school days.

I loved running track and feeling a sense of freedom while the cool wind hugged my face. After school, when Mom was working, I would join her in the kiosk, and I even learned how to roll the tobacco and make handmade cigars and cigarettes. Whenever we had the money and time we would go to the movie house, the theater or the opera. I learned a lot about art, music and drama. And yet life was lonely and terribly isolated.

When I turned thirteen, Mom and I moved to a new place, and I entered a very special school. It was actually a dorm for teenagers. We took regular classes and did our homework. The classes were either in the morning or in the afternoon. Before or after school we had to work. At first I was hired to do some ironing. Afterwards I collected tomatoes from the fields nearby, and then I gathered chicken eggs and milked cows. They also taught me the correct way to pick grapes and apples.

Summer break came, and we were granted a one-month vacation. Mom was working in a restaurant now. She actually helped the owner to run and manage it, besides supervising the cooks and the takeout counter. The owner of the restaurant let my mom rent a room in their big old house, located within walking distance of the ocean. She would visit me once a week in the dorm, but now, with my month away just around the corner, she was busy getting the place ready for my arrival.

Needless to say, I looked forward to getting away, going to the beach and doing nothing for a change. At thirteen I already knew what hard work was all about. I also knew about discipline, waking up very early in the morning and going to bed just before midnight.

Mom picked me up on Tuesday, and I had my little suitcase packed and ready to leave. We took the local city-to-city bus. It seemed that the ride took forever. I was anxious to get to the house I had heard so much about.

"The beach is right there," my mother said to me. "You walk down about thirty steps, and you are walking on sand."

I was thrilled. The sand and the salty ocean air sounded so good to me.

We arrived in the early afternoon. I unpacked my belongings, and without a thought I put on my sandals and walked down to the beach. I can still remember the meeting between the beach and me. This was my first trip to the beach, and within minutes I felt at ease. The sound of the ocean waves was mesmerizing. I sat on the sand and just listened and watched the swimmers, the kids running around and the parents preparing fruit. This was a completely unfamiliar world to me. Instantly I loved the place and felt so fortunate to be there. It was magical.

Little did I know that my dream would be shattered by Saturday afternoon.

On that day we sat down to eat lunch with the owner of the restaurant, his wife and two young boys, ages five and eight. I felt so mature and such an adult compared to those kids. I ate quickly, enjoying the egg salad sandwich with cucumbers on white bread and the glass of orange juice that my mother had prepared for me.

We all finished eating around 1 p.m., and everyone got up from the table and helped collect the dishes and clean up. Mom went into the kitchen with the owner's wife to wash the dishes and the two boys ran back to their room to play some kind of game. I walked over to the large bay window. It had a view of the ocean.

As I stood there, I felt slow footsteps approaching.

A very uncomfortable feeling came over me. As I turned, I saw a man with shining eyes staring at me in an odd way. Before I could turn around completely, he placed one of his hands firmly on my adolescent breast. The other hand started pulling off my little skirt. I tried to break away. That is when he pulled so hard on my T-shirt that it tore. Because of my great running ability I was able to get away. While I screamed for my mom, I ran out of the house with one sandal on my foot, a torn white T-shirt and a pulled-down skirt.

I will never forget how fast I ran at that moment. It felt like flying, and within minutes I was several blocks away, shouting for my mother. She also run down the stairs but did not have a clue about what had really happened to me. When she realized where the screaming came from, she found me. By then I was crying uncontrollably, and when I saw my mom's pale face I realized that we were in serious trouble.

Later on, I learned that the man who had tried to rape me—right there in the middle of the day, while his entire family and my mother were home—had raped other little girls in town. Perhaps they were not such good runners. When his first son turned thirteen, the man committed suicide.

After my mother and I calmed down, we sat together on the beach sand. Then we suddenly realized that we did not have our belongings with us. We had no money and no home to go back to.

We walked to the police station and told them the story. They sent an officer out to collect our stuff, but the man in the house would not open the door for them. Mom and I ended up sleeping on the floor in an old lady's house nearby. She gave us some cold grapes, a few slices of bread and a glass of water for dinner.

We stayed with the lady for the next three weeks. During all that time, we had only the clothes we had worn that day. We ate fruits and vegetables left on the produce stands after the local market closed. The bakery gave us rolls they could not sell. Basically we had bread, water, grapes and plums for three weeks. We received our belongings at the end of the third week, and by then I had to get ready to go back to the dorm.

I was worried about Mom. Where would she go? Where would she land her next job? And when would we have a home life again?

With great luck, Mom met a very nice gentleman. Another man, who sat on a bench reading his paper in the local park, introduced him to her. While sitting there, he had overheard my mother's bitter crying and came up with the idea of introducing her to a respectable widower.

They got married six months later, and when I had the opportunity to come home I turned over a completely new leaf in my life.

Even though I now lived in a nice, spacious home with lots of orange trees around us, ate good food and wore lovely clothes and shoes, I was still insecure and shy and felt completely isolated from the rest of the world.

I cried myself to sleep most nights and especially on weekends. I would watch other girls and boys my age go out to a party or a movie or just walk up and down the avenue, while I stayed at home playing cards with my mother or watching something on television. I was too protected, too sheltered and perhaps loved and cared for too much. I did not feel confident, and I certainly did not think that I was pretty or someone with whom others wanted to socialize.

I remember so clearly the feelings I had: a longing, aching wish to be noticed and to belong.

On the night that Mom finally gave me permission to go to a party with two of my school friends, I felt joy in my heart, along with anxiety about what to do. How should I behave? And would I meet a boy to my liking? Fortunately I did. He and I became close friends. He was five years older. I was 17 and he was not quite 22, about to graduate from college as an engineer.

I fell completely into him. The expression on my face and my deep brown eyes that longed for closeness revealed my innermost desires, and without speaking a word I captured him. I was thin, pale and extremely unaware of my femininity. We had an instant chemistry with each other, and the following week he came over to the house to take me out to a movie. I could not believe that he took several hours on his day off from school just to see me.

We went out for a couple of months, until Mom expressed serious concerns about our relationship and made me promise to stop seeing him. Of course I gave in to her plea, and my heart sank deeper than I ever thought it could. I became even more closed-in and depressed than before. I had very little desire to do anything besides going to school and seeing a couple of my girlfriends once a month or so.

I felt parental control taking a stranglehold on me. I decided that the best choice would be for me to get out of the house as a respectable young woman and marry the first boy who seemed serious and decent.

And so I did. I met my first husband, who was nine years older, and we got married about three months after we met. He was good to me and expressed genuine care and tremendous love and affection. But I was a young woman not quite 18 years old, and the spark I once felt for him ceased to exist. I liked the young man, but there was no passion in my heart for him, and we had very little chemistry between us.

Only a few weeks after the wedding, I realized what I had done. But it was too late. I was a married woman expecting our first child. I lost the baby, but I knew deep inside that I did not possess the maturity to be a mother or even a wife.

I left our home and moved back to my mother's place. I was confused and terribly upset and felt completely out of sync. For nine months I continued living in my mother's home while I saw my husband occasionally. He truly loved me in his own way, but I cared less.

During those months I went out a few times, but it was always the same feeling when I came home: empty, isolated, lacking confidence. Every time I looked in the mirror I felt unattractive and not very exciting.

I went back with my husband, understanding that it was the best thing to do at the time. The relationship was acceptable. He gave as much as he could, and I took as much as I wanted.

I gained a tremendous amount of weight, replacing love with food, and I felt even more unwanted. I had no desire to buy clothes or dress up. I had no enthusiasm for anything but working, going to school and saving my money. Occasionally we would get together with the friends he had before the wedding, but most of the time we went to see a movie or to eat at his parents' house or my mother's home.

The lack of joy turned me in another direction. I stopped eating regularly, and when I did I made myself vomit right after. I rejected food just as much as I rejected the poor relationship I was experiencing.

Looking back with the maturity and understanding I have today, I know that all the decisions I made and the feelings I experienced then felt right at the time. I did not know any better, and I did not have anyone in my life with whom I could share my bitter emotions. My mother was too controlling and demanding. She used to say, "You deserve it. I am the best mother around. I have done so much for you. My life was more difficult than yours. I am a better and wiser person than you." And as close as we were, I did not feel the freedom and the courage to speak up or try to change anything. I followed her wishes completely, feeling guilty if I even thought otherwise. My husband was totally smothering me. He was not very talkative or expressive. He was not raised that way either and lacked confidence as well. No wonder we connected. He was also more mature, and I never felt that he could validate my emotions. So I decided to keep the doors to my heart closed. It was safer and less eventful.

I preferred to talk to no one about the many things that bothered me. I watched other couples look at one another with different eyes, holding hands or just completely glued to one another. When I saw a kiss of passion on screen, I only wished that I were the one instead of the actress playing the role.

◆   ◆   ◆

A few years went by, and I had many more troubled moments and made many more poor decisions and choices.

And then a big change came into my life. I was pregnant again. This time I was ready to have a child and be a mother. As soon as I heard the news, I felt not only ecstatic but totally delighted and content.

As the due date moved closer, my baby and I connected in a very special way. I talked to him, and I felt love. His presence inside my belly showered me with tenderness, exuberance and complete joy. Isn't it amazing how an unborn baby can create such a change in one's feelings and attitude toward life?

When I gave birth to my son, I began to open up from my isolation. The moment I saw him I expressed joyful emotions with a loud cry and such a happy heart. I was grateful and began to smile and speak to the people around me. Giving birth to a nine-and-a-half-pound baby seemed like nothing at all. It is funny how we perceive the most difficult moments in our lives when we feel uplifted and cheerful.

From that day on, I waved differently to people on the streets. I stopped and talked a few moments with neighbors while pushing the stroller. When I entered the local grocery store, I smiled. Everywhere I went I felt confident and positive. People would ask me, "Why are you smiling so gracefully? Did you win the lotto? What is the great thing that happened to you?" I would answer: "Life, and I am so grateful to be a mother. I have a son now and with his arrival I opened my heart." That's wonderful," they would say. "Good luck to you."

And that is how I started to develop relationships. I became much more talkative, more inquisitive, more interested in others and more open to listening. Very soon I made new friends. People wanted to be around me as a magnetism grew between us.

Life was never the same again. I was communicating. I was connecting with family members, friends, coworkers, neighbors, salespeople and children. The void of my loneliness and that sunken feeling I always had were being replaced by a bubbly personality with a big, wide smile and shiny, deep-brown eyes that spoke without words.

The world had a completely new color. I found myself becoming extremely helpful to others, ready to give unconditionally when I detected vulnerability or weakness. Now I was a pillar of strength, demonstrating my support without ego or the desire to control. This is how I began my first baby steps toward building relationships, and I climbed higher and higher as time went by.

Now let me share with you Lea's story about relationships.

5

Lea and I worked together at a bank overseas. It was my second job and Lea's first. She was born in Bulgaria and her parents immigrated to my country when she was three years old. To them it seemed like a very logical decision. Lea's father had a great job offer as a mechanical engineer in a large factory. It was a solid opportunity for him; he would make more money, and Lea's mother could stay home with her while she was pregnant with their second daughter.

The change was great for this young couple and the "surprise" baby girl; for Lea, however, the new place painted a dark and unpleasant picture. Back in Bulgaria, Lea and her parents lived in a small home behind her grandmother's house. The main house had two stories. The grandparents lived on the ground floor, and Lea's uncle lived on the top floor with his wife, a baby boy and a little girl Lea's age. Her name was Blanca, and Lea loved playing with her from the very first day she began to crawl. Lea and Blanca were inseparable.

So when Lea's parents moved to the small apartment in the new place, Lea felt terribly uncomfortable, and the unfamiliar surroundings saddened her deeply. But the worst moment came when she screamed out loud over and over again, "Blanca! Blanca! Come and play with me!" and there was no response. The memory of Blanca became a fading picture in her mind, a memory of the past delicately engraved into her tiny heart.

Lea stopped eating. She experienced lots of nightmares, and the happy little girl turned into a sad grownup, sitting in the

corner of her room holding her favorite doll—named Blanca—
and looking at the ceiling. Her parents grew very concerned and
took Lea to the local pediatrician for a checkup. They told him
about the relocation and the changes in Lea. She missed her
cousin and friend Blanca terribly.

The doctor understood her emotional state of mind and pro-
posed two options. The first was to have her parents meet with
the local neighbors and seek new playmates for Lea, preferably
little girls close to her age. That should help her get over Blanca,
he explained. The second choice was to send her back to her
grandparents for a month or so, the result being that she would
miss her parents and ask to return to her new home.

Her parents chose the second option.

So, with a sad heart and a troubled mind, Lea's father took
her on the night train to begin the journey back to their old
home. When they got there, Lea was so thrilled to see Blanca's
face that she even forgot to wave good-bye to her father and
greet the rest of the family. She was happy, and she jumped up
and down like a new yo-yo.

An entire month went by, and Lea never asked to go back to
her parents' house. The family became very concerned. By that
time Lea was eating better and sleeping all night.

She stayed there for two more months. One week after Lea's
mother gave birth to a sister, Avoria, her uncle took her back
home to her parents' house. They were all optimistic, hoping
that when she met her baby sister she would be totally happy
and forget that she had left Blanca and the old house.

But reality came in a very different shape. Lea cried through
the whole trip back home. When she was introduced to her

baby sister she walked away, saying, "I do not like her. She is ugly and so small. I want to go back to my old home!"

Lea grew up to be a very thin, pale, shy and isolated young girl. She was never close to her sister, and when she turned 16 she got on a bus and took the trip back to her uncle's house without telling her parents. She reconnected with Blanca, as if time had stood still for the 13 years they were separated. She stayed there for the whole summer. They played guitar together, giggled and laughed at boys, ate lots of ice cream and walked long hours by the beach. Those were great days for Lea. But they ended the very first week in September, when she had to return home.

The school year started all over again. Lea hated school, her 13-year-old sister and her parents, who had taken her away from Blanca and the place she loved so much.

Lea barely graduated high school. Her passion was the guitar and flamenco music. She had no desire to go to college and learn a trade. She stayed home. She preferred not to go out any-where and made no friends. Her life was simple. She focused on her guitar, her music and her photo album with so many great memories of the time she had spent with Blanca.

Then, one month before her 18th birthday, something tragic happened.

Her mother was diagnosed with lung cancer. Lea felt com-pletely detached from the news. She had a great deal of anger in her, and she had never forgiven her parents for moving. Her mother passed away about three months later, and Lea and her sister were on their own. Her father spent long hours at work; it was his escape from cruel reality. He had loved his wife, but he could not deal with the trauma. He would come home, eat a slice of bread with something on it, take a shower and go to bed. It was a routine, and the girls and he exchanged few words. They had no communication, only feelings of anger and despair.

A month after her mom passed away, Lea saw a small sign in the bank window: LOOKING FOR A FILING CLERK. She applied and the position was hers.

We met on her second day on the job, and somehow we felt a certain closeness. We were both just the same: closed, shy and terribly insecure.

Once in a while we spoke, but only for work reasons. Sometimes we would say good-night at the end of the day.

I left the bank several weeks before I gave birth to my son. Lea stayed there. She was 22 at the time and I was almost 23, married and very much expecting.

Three years went by. On a cloudy afternoon just one week before my son's third birthday, I ran into her in the open produce and flower market. I loved to go there for shopping. Everything was fresh, so presentable and quite delicious. I did not notice her at first but the voice behind me seemed so familiar. I looked back and it was Lea. She was holding hands with a nice-looking young gentleman. She recognized me right away and we looked at each other with surprise and acknowledgment. Lea spoke first.

"Come here," she said, "and meet my husband. This is Michael." He extended a warm hand to me.

"I am Ana," I said with a big smile. "Lea and I used to work together.":

"I see," he replied.

"By the way," Lea said, "do you have time for a coffee?" I was stunned by the offer. We never had coffee or lunch or a snack together. *What an idea*, I thought to myself. But, as if she were reading my mind, she added with pride, "I have a story to tell you. Come, let's sit down. I know a great coffee shop right around the corner. The pastry there is superb." She said it with such confidence.

And so Lea, her husband Michael, my three-year-old son and I went to the coffee shop.

That was when I learned her childhood story and how the relocation had affected her those many years ago.

"You seem so content and full of life now," I said to her as I sipped my hot cappuccino.

"Yes." She rested her head on her husband's shoulder for a moment. "You see, Ana, Michael is Rony's brother. And Rony is Blanca's husband."

"What I miracle!" I exclaimed. "This is so amazing!" Blanca and Ron had met on a farm vacation, and they got married shortly after. At the wedding Lea met Michael. They connected at once. Now the two couples lived only a few blocks from each other. Lea could not have been happier.

I saw her a year later, walking with twins down the main boulevard, next to a lovely young woman with dark brown hair and black eyes who held a beautiful baby girl of her own in her arms. It was Blanca. We chatted for a while. Lea could not stop talking about her new home, the twins and the promotion her husband had received as a professor at the local university. We became close friends and got together quite often.

After my family immigrated to the United States, I never saw Lea again. But I remembered her words of wisdom to me: "You will do just fine. You are great in relationships, and that is half of the secret of success."

She was absolutely right.

6

Albert was a troubled teenager. He was overweight and his curly reddish hair did not look very attractive to others. His skin showed the transition from childhood to adulthood. He was not popular at school and had no friends whatsoever.

His father was busy with his job. He was the head of the household and, with no education or training in a specific trade, he worked various odd jobs, driving produce from town to town, running a cleaning service and guarding a large warehouse far away from home. Albert's mother had to stretch their limited paycheck to feed a family of four.

Albert had a sister a few years older than he was. His mother baked homemade bread and cookies for the neighborhood children to generate extra income, washed the family's clothes and kept the house clean. She also grew vegetables in their small garden and made fresh jam and homemade pickles every year. She kept a very busy schedule, so both parents had very little time to spend with their two children. Albert's sister got into trouble at the age of 16, and her 18-year-old boyfriend married her as soon as he found out that she was expecting. They moved away to a small farming town where the boy's parents grew corn and lettuce.

As the only child at home, Albert felt hundreds of generations removed from his parents. He had no desire to talk to them about anything at all.

Until one special day changed everything.

On a beautiful, sunny summer morning, Albert woke up from a strangely disturbing dream. Even though the day looked bright and promising, his heart and mind felt disturbed and very lonely. It was 6 a.m. when he looked at the small clock on the bedroom wall. He got up quickly and walked over to his bathroom. He brushed his teeth without looking in the mirror, preferring not to see the reflection of his face. He washed and took a speedy shower. Then he pulled on an old pair of jeans and a dark blue T-shirt, faded after so many washings, and put on a pair of open-toed sandals. He walked out to the street without breakfast and did not bother to leave a note for his parents, who were still sleeping.

It was Sunday. The streets were quiet and peaceful, but he was not. The message in the dream bothered him deeply. He had been all by himself on a small island in the middle of nowhere. The ocean waves were hitting hard and high and the island trees were swaying.

"Is anyone else here besides me?" Albert shouted.

All he could hear was the echo of his own words. He sat down beside a large old tree and stared at the big red rock facing him. He was all alone, and the feeling was overwhelming and incredibly real. After shouting out again and again for help, he finally woke up.

Now, walking the familiar streets of his town, he was able to relate more easily to his feelings and reactions in the dream.

He knew he no longer wanted to be alone. The deserted island dream had affected him vividly and intensely. How could he change his looks? And how would he invite new people into his life? It was a dilemma, and he had no one to share his concerns about the challenge.

Albert must have walked for hours before noticing that he was no longer in town. Now he was walking on an open road with no pavement, no cars driving by, no homes and no people in sight. He stopped as fear began to fill him. He breathed faster and faster. Within seconds he felt his body go weak and he fell down on the rough, rocky ground.

A soft, gentle voice spoke to him with slow, kind words: "Let me get you up.".

Albert opened his eyes. A tall man stood over him with open arms, ready to pull him to his feet. Albert got up shakily, feeling lightheaded.

"It's okay," the man said. "You must have passed out. Perhaps you need to eat something. My name is Doctor Collins. And what is your name, young man?" He had a very caring voice.

"My name is Albert."

"Well, it's so nice to meet you, Albert. You see, my car drove over a large rock, and I have a flat. But I also have some bananas and juice with me. Let me give you something to eat, and afterwards perhaps you can help me change the tire."

They walked to the car, which was only a few feet away. Albert was speechless and his legs felt like rubber. The doctor handed him a banana and a small can of orange juice. Albert took them without hesitation and started to bite into the banana. As soon as he finished the fruit and the juice he felt a sudden rush in his head, along with renewed energy.

The doctor and Albert changed the tire together, working slowly and deliberately. The sun beat hard on their backs and they had no shade around them. They were both tired and sweating after the task. There were no cell phones in those days, and the area was completely deserted on a Sunday morning.

With the spare tire on the car, the doctor offered Albert a ride back into town. The boy accepted, nodding his head. They rode together without a word. The doctor seemed to understood him better than Albert did himself.

As they came to Albert's street, the boy pointed and said with a low voice, "My home is right there, the one with the blue roof and the green fence around it."

"I see," the doctor said. "Then we are almost there." He stopped the car, and as Albert put his hand on the door handle the doctor asked him a serious question. "How would you like to come with me to Africa, Albert? I can use your help. You see, I am leaving next week to improve health care there. I am going to a very small village where there will be lots of children and teenagers. A group of doctors from other countries will join me. I think you might enjoy the experience."

Albert was speechless. He did not understand how the doctor had figured him out so easily, how he knew that he was so disconnected from his parents. *He must be a very intelligent, kind man*, he thought, and without waiting another minute to digest the proposal, Albert accepted it with a broad smile. It sounded incredibly exciting and interesting. He remembered an old movie he had seen the year before, about a family living in Africa, and the memory remained with him.

"I will go with you," Albert told him, honored.

"Okay," said the doctor. "I am so glad that you accepted my invitation. There is only one more thing we must do." He looked intently at Albert's face. "I must ask your parents for their permission. You are not quite an adult as of yet. Anyhow, it is only for a couple of months. I will bring you back home before the school year begins."

Albert felt anxious and asked the doctor to come in with him right now and meet his parents.

Dr. Collins entered their home, walking behind Albert. His parents were sitting in front of the television set in the living room, eating their breakfast on separate trays. The did not ask Albert where he had been. The doctor seemed to understand the situation. He asked confidently if he could sit down. The parents were a bit intimidated by the man's appearance, but they nodded their heads and motioned for him to sit on the large couch. Albert sat down beside him.

The doctor's request was granted without many questions. Albert felt happier than he could ever remember.

Two days later, he packed for his adventure, looking forward to new surroundings and a life he new nothing about.

◆   ◆   ◆

This was Albert's first important relationship with people outside of his family, and in unfamiliar territory to boot. He felt important and needed. He became very comfortable with the natives and the rest of the medical crew. Everyone liked him, and he was so occupied helping with the various chores that he did not notice he was losing quite a bit of weight. His skin got a dark tan color and his curly red hair got lighter, shining like pure gold in the sun. His blue-green eyes shone like the clearest sapphires.

Albert was a new boy.

He arrived home just in time to get ready for school. His parents barely recognized him. He greeted his neighbors, his teachers and his schoolmates with a cheerful smile on his face. He told everyone about his experiences in Africa and how much he had learned there. How wonderful it was to help people in need, people who were so much less fortunate.

He and the doctor remained friends for a long, long time.

When Albert graduated from high school he was at the top of his class, and his grades earned him a full scholarship to a medical school. He knew what he wanted to do for the rest of his life. He was passionate about it. His desire to help children topped the list. He wanted to become a pediatrician, and so he did. He completed medical school one year earlier than his classmates. Immediately upon receiving his diploma, he followed up with an internship in Africa.

It was even more delightful the second time around. Children he had helped were now grown up and had kids of their own. Albert developed strong bonds and fine relationships built on care, love, attention, respect and support. He was never alone again. He completed his internship with a fulfilled heart, knowing that he had changed people's lives. Thinking back, he realized what a turn his own life had taken, and all because of a chance occurrence.

Albert was offered several positions, and he accepted one in a small town next to where he had grown up. There he met his bride. She was the head nurse in the surgical center. Laura was a lovely girl with straight, chestnut-colored hair and deep jade-green eyes. She had an olive complexion and a delightful personality. Their relationship grew steadily and solidly. They knew how to nourish the seed for a long-lasting, loving union.

Within four years, the couple had two boys and a girl. Albert loved his children and he loved his wife. On Sunday mornings he would cook breakfast for all of them. They ate together slowly and talked for hours. Albert knew how to connect and be involved in his children's lives. It came easy for him. He had learned all about relationships.

We can draw relationships in every shape and color, but we should never overlook their value and importance in all areas of our lives.

PART II

"Time Life Love Time Original Formula"

Well, I have been in the same place as many of you are now. I felt overwhelmed with duties at home, responsibilities at work and life itself. I juggled more than my mind could absorb, my body was tired, and I was only 35 years old at the time. My perception was that I was going nowhere. I had no achievement of any kind to show. My financial situation was not secure and I was alone, without a husband or a partner.

Basically I did not feel successful or contented with my life, and the direction I was taking did not seem particularly promising or exciting. I also felt a sense of dependency, and I lacked self-esteem and self-confidence. In so many words, I felt lost and detached and sensed that I was running out of time to make something more of myself.

My daily existence was devoid of enthusiasm. I was working at least 60 hours a week, including weekends, as a financial executive for a large corporation. I was a single mother to a teenage boy, and my own mother lived with us, so I had to make time for them, too. I felt a deep, loving obligation to spend quality moments with these very special people in my life, and I put myself last on the list.

But where was I? Where was the time for my personal goals, my dreams and my relationship with myself? The latter was failing. I had no time for myself. After doing all of the chores, the errands, the paperwork, in addition to a daily two-to three-hour drive to and from work—and more—I had no time to relax and just "be." Several months after my 35th birthday, with so much on my plate to deal with, I fell apart. That was the day I found out my father had passed away in Europe.

I knew I had to make changes, but where was I going to cut back or cut down? Then another blow came along. My mother was diagnosed with breast cancer, and she needed my help at home. That was when I realized I must make some changes in my life and understand reality. I reduced my working hours and spent more time with my family, especially my mother. It was a decision forced by destiny, but nevertheless it was a helpful one. Mom got better.

At the time I had the hope that everything else would fall into place without my lifting a finger. But it did not.

I came to the realization that I had to make a solid, organized plan for my personal and home life. I had to list on a sheet of paper my short-term goals and my long-term dreams. I was aware that a solid, well-organized plan at work would help me accomplish more, and that I could improve my personal life with the extra time I spent with my family and myself. For the next couple of months I made some progress, but I was still not satisfied.

Time was going by too quickly.

As I found myself caught up in the stream of life, I came to realize that the only energy to keep me moving forward was the plan. When would I buy I new car? When would I meet Mr. Right? Would my son graduate? When could I purchase a home? And of course at the age of 36 you worry about your appearance, so I was always looking forward to the next new outfit, shoes, purse or jewelry. I had the idea in mind that someday I would be able to purchase designer clothing and other luxury items for my family and myself, without any concern for the checkbook. So here it was: always the plan, the next project, the next thing, and so on and on.

I called this the destination.

When? Where? How? I had something that kept me going until tomorrow, but what about the next day and the next one? I forgot to live in the now. And time came and went without breaks. It took several major challenges in my personal life to shake me up even further. I had to make some choices with or without the desire for change.

On a very cool, rainy Sunday morning, an idea woke me up and got me out of bed. I began thinking about my relationship with time and came up with the following list:

- I must learn how to live in the now.

- I need to extract the seed of experience from yesterday—time past.

- I have to enjoy using time.

- I can accomplish more with time.

- I can fall in love with time.

- I can appreciate time and everything I can do with it.

- I can learn not to ignore time.

- And, most of all, I can respect time and accept its power without controlling it. I need to understand the relationship between time and myself.

Whoa! I felt that I was going somewhere with this. As I started to think differently, I began to feel differently about time. We became the best of friends. Time became a fantastic companion. As I began moving forward with this new understanding, I realized that I was making some progress. But after a month or so, I stopped myself and got off the track as a big question popped into my head. It was a good one, touching base with reality and introducing some common sense to my new discovery. The question was this:

Why does this seem so easy for me?

I was becoming comfortable with the process, but I needed to think of other people, too. How could I teach others to apply this program, make it easy and fun, and create the desire within each and every individual to pursue this program?

That is when I started researching time usage in the past. As I looked back to the eighteenth century, I stumbled into some very interesting material. I called it "The Power of Hats" or, more precisely, "The Ancient Wisdom of Hats." The ancients used various types of hats of different shapes and fabrics to represent an individual's status, respect, power, friendship or enemies. One would wear the appropriate hat at the proper time and place in order to deliver a specific message. Sometimes the messenger would take it off and put it on a piece of furniture or hold it in the right or left hand.

How exactly did it work?

As I continued my research, a light bulb seemed to turn on. I smiled as everything cleared up and fell into place.

I began to practice the hat game on my own, and within one month's time I came up with a complete formula, enjoying every step of the way. I incorporated the ancient wisdom of hats into my time management formula and styled the two together, tailoring the method to fit today's reality as we choose to live it. Vintage is in! It all made perfect sense.

Now I invite you to join me in this incredible adventure. You will have fun with the program. You can play games with it. And, most importantly, you can release stress while you learn how to build and improve your own all-important relationship with time.

So start smiling. You are already on the right track. I am delighted that you have chosen to spend your time with me and read this simple but powerful program.

Thank you!

ANA H.B. WEBER

Introduction

Let me ask you a few questions and introduce some concepts. These will stimulate your mind and awaken a new awareness to help you face the facts. You will then understand that there is room for learning how to manage time and how to apply this formula in your day-to-day life. You've got time, so let's begin.

- What does time represent to you?

- What do you do with it?

- Can you purchase it for a price?

- Can you exchange it for another product?

- Can you reverse time?

- Can you go back in time?

- Can you stop time?

- Can you see time?

- Do you touch time?

- Do you feel time?

- Do you appreciate time?

- Do you respect time?

- Do you acknowledge the power of time?

- Do you love time?

- Do you hear yourself say, "I don't have enough time"?

Here are some statements that may seem all too familiar to you:

- I cannot do it all with the time I have.

- It seems that I accomplish so little with time—and *on* time.

- I wish I had more time. I need more than 24 hours in a day to do it all.

- I jump from one thing to another and nothing seems to get done right.

- I want to do so much, like going back to school, making more money and having more time for the things I like.

- I do not want to be preoccupied with so many things that I do not enjoy doing.

- I am always rushing from point A to point B, and time just seems to fly by.

- I must get this done by a certain date, and only so much time is left.

The list could go on and on. These are all realistic and normal feelings and expressions. But we live in a fast-paced world. It seems that the hands on the clock turn more rapidly as time goes by. As we get older, we feel that time passes faster and there is no space between events. Only during the childhood years does it seem that time moves slowly; we wish we were grownups already and could be treated like adults. When we are six going on seven, we say that we are six-and-a-half, and so on, until we pass the teenage years. After that we focus more on the smaller number.

So many people out there never admit their true age, and you have to wonder why. Are they embarrassed by how they look? What have they accomplished in their lives? Are they afraid of tomorrow, of acknowledging the fact that they have so many years behind them and so few that remain ahead, according to statistics? Perhaps they want to look youthful and be treated that way. It could be all of the above.

We have to keep in mind that time will move forward, and so will we. So many new programs and ideas and tools and drugs and nutritional products are on the marketplace today, claiming to make you feel younger, look younger and help you "turn back the clock." The truth is that they can only go so far. Time is still ahead of us, and we simply cannot change that.

Therefore we must accept the facts of life and reality. What can we do about it?

We cannot control time. We would love to manipulate it and treat it in the same way as other commodities, tools and products. Wouldn't we like to exercise an option to buy time? Does time have a price tag? Can we create an opportunity to exchange time for a new toy that we want? On occasion we contemplate going back in time, or we try to replace time with other ideas and actions. Can a makeover turn back time? Could we give time itself a makeover, make it look younger and more attractive, move more slowly and be more fit? Can we expand the 24-hour day to 36?

Obviously all of the above are completely impossible. So let's consider the choices we have and what we can do with time.

SEGMENT ONE:

Reality—Today—Living in the Now!

Reality

People of all ages face the realities of time.

Children:

- They need to get up on time and be on time for school.

- They must brush their teeth, wash their faces, get dressed and of course eat some breakfast.

- Kids already feel rushed. How often do parents say, "Get out of bed! You need to be ready for school in half an hour. I must drop you off as early as I can so I am not late for work." Sound familiar?

- Yes, the routine is repeated five days a week. What happens after school?

- The same all over again, but even more so. You have to go to soccer practice, swimming lessons, ballet, music and so on.

- And then comes homework, dinner, a little TV, a game or a bit of outdoor fun, though kids today spend very little time outside.

- Next is bath time and getting ready for bed until tomorrow, when the same plan repeats again.

- The weekend brings little relief. There are birthday parties for friends, perhaps some homework for Monday, and clean-up time.

- You try to go to church and have some special time with family and grandparents.

Teenagers:

- Teenagers have so little time for doing anything at all, which is a desire they build within the social circles they surround themselves with.

- They have homework, part-time jobs, driver's education, all the while looking forward to more independence. Then they have their social activities and forbidden love games.

- Just like the little kids, they have to clean up the messes in their rooms.

- Of course their parents want them to apply to colleges and universities so they can get a good education and become productive members of society.

- What teenager can escape getting yelled at by parents? "Why do you look so terrible? We need to get a haircut for you, Tim! I don't want you to pick baggy clothes anymore. And those colors! Stop using the cell phone all the time. You have to get away from that computer screen. Why is your door always closed? You must be home by ten. Jessica, you're too young for makeup. You need to wear different T-shirts. And you are not allowed to go out with boys until you're sixteen!"

- Time and again, teenagers try to get out of doing their chores and the activities they don't like, including homework. And they resent being told to do such things.

- Teenagers would rather spend time doing things that fit their immature desires, like going to the mall, chatting on the telephone, eating out, driving around aimlessly, going to the movies, competing with other kids about how they look, or bragging about new body piercings and tattoos on their soft young skin.

Adults:

- Well, how much is truly expected of us? Lots. In fact, everything!

- We have to go to work, or juggle work and school at the same time.

- We have the pressure and stress of deadlines, often worrying about how to keep a job that we do not feel passionate about in the first place; we need to survive, and change seems too scary.

- We spend inordinate amounts of time managing our personal finances, too much time at work, and too little time on fun.

- We strive to keep our commitments to our partners. "When are you going to be home, honey? I need to have dinner ready …"

- I need to go shopping, but first I have to stop by the dry cleaners on the way. Then I realize that my car is out of gas.

Of course my mood is even darker, because gas prices are not what they used to be.

- If we have kids, there are additional responsibilities that need our time after work. We must drive them to their various activities, and to purchase school supplies—including new tennis shoes, because they grow so quickly.

- When we arrive home, most of the day is gone. Time did not stop for a second. We glance at the large clock on the wall, realizing that it's already close to 6 p.m. and dinner is nowhere in sight.

- Our kids need help with their homework. By the time they go to bed, we do not know if we should calm down from the day's activities by taking a hot bath, watching a television show or listening to some music.

- In the best of cases, some couples help one another after work with the kids and the chores around the house.

- Today's reality is that in most cases, we need two incomes to keep up with the lifestyles we choose to live and to get more toys with which to fill our already limited time.

- In some cases the breadwinner has a significantly large income, so the other parent can choose to stay home with the kids. But even then the parent at home seems to be busy most of the time, feeling that there is not enough time to accomplish half the chores.

- Let us also not forget those individuals who frequently need to travel away from home. Salespeople, marketing representatives, contract negotiators, engineers, builders, designers, actors, producers, buyers and executives are often on the go. They seem to accomplish even less with the little time they have left after returning home, tired and burned-out from keeping their careers at full speed. Where does one find the time to exercise or go out for a quiet dinner? Who is going to play with the kids? Just when can one get away from stress and responsibilities in general?

These problems and challenges are amplified for **single parents.**

- Their stress level is even deeper. At times they need to fill in for the financial expectations of two. How much time and energy do they expend figuring out how to get back at and punish their exes? They have to spend more time (and money) than they would like on attorneys. How can they get more out of the separation instead of living in the past?

- As we all know, reality is simply there. We cannot change the cosmic spinning of time. We cannot live yesterday; that time is gone forever. And we cannot change the events of yesterday. We made what we thought were the best choices at the time, and we have to move on in spite of the consequences.

Now what steps can we take to implement change with time—something so desperately needed?

1. Learn to accept the time spent on yesterday as a seed of experience.

2. We need to apply the key technique of detaching ourselves from yesterday by separating thinking in the past from thinking in the now.

3. We need to release the clutter from yesterday, which represents time past. For example, could we buy the year 2000 for $1 million in 2006? Certainly not. Then why buy, lease or rent the events and feelings of yesterday? We do—but we must undo that!

4. We must focus on the now. This is the time for now—today.

5. Cherish the time that is gone. It was a free gift to you. Leave it that way.

6. You can do all you desire with your time now.

7. Plant the idea with strong, lasting roots in your mind, then follow it up with action.

8. Visualize a scale and place each of these mental products on it, as follows:

   a. On the left side: positive, constructive, light, fun and promising activities—those that feel right just by looking at them.

   b. On the right side: negative, destructive, heavy, dull activities full of uncertainty—those that feel wrong just by looking at them.

      • Which side will you choose? Why not the alternative?

- Stop and practice the scale game every time you face a challenge or have choices to make.

- First look to the middle and pick no side at all.

- Watch the scale.

- Consider that to someone else the event in question might not be a challenge, but to you it is.

- Respect and validate your feelings.

- Learn and understand your choices, your life, your decisions and your actions.

- Do not react too quickly to an adverse situation.

- Let the space flow in and deal with it later.

- Be proactive instead. Would you not rather see clearer and more significant results?

- Release the stress that way. You are ready to deal with the next thing.

  - Concentrate on the now.

  - Practice the now.

  - Feel the now.

  - Enjoy the now.

  - Block out everything else.

  - Focus on the now.

  - Think of the now.

  - Believe in the now.

- Smile in the now.

- Deal with the now.

- Do not question the now; it will always be there for you.

- Remember: time does not stop, but you can expand the now.

- Acknowledge the now.

- Respect the now.

- Love the now.

- Recognize the now.

- Use now wisely.

- You will see immediate results in the now.

- You will become calmer and less anxious.

- You will not be so overwhelmed with responsibilities "outside the fence" in the now.

- You will become a more exciting person to be around, more enthused and passionate about every step you take.

- Life is like a string of pearls on a silk thread—each pearl shines singularly and together they become the complete piece. A pearl cannot stand on its own, unless it is held in place by a tool and then carefully attached to a garment, a fabric or a piece of jewelry.

THE SECRET CODE

- Start with ten minutes a day (there are 1,440 minutes in a day). At the same time every day for 30 days, DO ABSOLUTELY NOTHING.

- Continue with ten minutes daily for the next 30 days. Write down the three most important things in your life: ideas, passions, purposes, goals, etc. Think about these and feel them.

- After you have spent ten minutes a day for 60 days—remember, always at the same time—begin to ACT on the feelings, ideas and goals you have written down.

- These baby steps will become a way of life. You will be surprised at how each 10-minute session expands. Soon there will be TIME FOR IT.

SEGMENT TWO:

Discipline—Organization—Order—Destinations

Discipline

- We learn at a young age what discipline is all about.

- Discipline is not an enemy! It is not stressful and should not be resented. It is actually a stress *releaser,* a friend and a helper in so many areas of our lives.

- When we apply discipline, we assign a specific level of acceptance to our responsibilities. By dealing with discipline and applying it every step of the way, we actually walk through our responsibilities. Discipline becomes a way of life.

- For example, we can all discipline ourselves to get out of bed 15 minutes earlier than we usually do. This extra quarter-hour will allow us to get ready for work without hurrying. When we drive to work, we won't have to rush as much. We will feel less anxiety while taking that quick shower and have a few minutes to drink our coffee sitting down instead of standing up.

- We can decide to get our clothes for tomorrow ready the night before.

- Since we are not in as much of a hurry, we can take our time and pick out clothing, shoes and accessories to fit the occasion—work, home, the gym, a tennis game, a breakfast meeting, a trip for the day or whatever.

- When we practice the way of discipline, we give ourselves an extra boost for the day to come.

- I can hear you asking, "How can I do all that and still live in the now? We block out experiencing the now." But we also have to use our common sense about making the now less stressful and more enjoyable.

- There is a fine art in understanding the now and time before and after it. Learn to recognize and differentiate the now from the past and the future.

Other Types of Discipline

- Prepare lunch for the kids the night before.

- If you bring lunch to work, prepare your own the night before.

- If you have an early meeting in the morning, confirm it via telephone the night before.

- Get your briefcase and all necessary paperwork ready the night before.

- If you are going to have a very busy, hectic day, do not eat too late in the evening, and do not make it a big meal.

- Apply the previous principle to drinking, even water.

- Do not get into a heated conversation with your partner or be confrontational the night before your big day.

- Put aside emotional and personal matters before going to bed. Let them rest and deal with them at the proper time, when everyone is calm, rested and more logical. The right time to deal with such issues is when the mood is uplifted and joyful.

- Do not ask yourself how to bring up the emotional or personal topic now. It will damage your momentum. On the contrary, the situation will be resolved in the proper fashion at the correct time and everyone will feel relieved.

- The best time to pursue negotiations is when you are experiencing less confrontation and conflict.

- Remember, time also encompasses *timing*. Everything has its own place and moment. Choose the proper time.

- Think before acting.

Organization

- Spend a few minutes every day organizing your room, your files and your belongings as you go. You will find your life a little lighter and less cluttered, and you will be able to think and act more clearly.

- Organize business and personal meetings well in advance, and give everyone adequate notice.

- Plan properly and respect time.

- Be congenial about schedule changes and reorganize.

- When you want to purchase a new house, remodel your existing home, buy a new car or make any other large capital expenditure, organize and make a plan before you begin.

Here are some ways to be organized:

- Prepare the plan by going over each step.

- Write down the steps.

- Think realistically, and assign a specific time and date for completing the project.

- Remember, time is the most expensive commodity.

- Do not waste everyone else's time when you are not certain about the task.

- Get your action list organized.

- Follow your plan with the support of others, and utilize their expertise in the areas needed.

- Organize your thinking.

- Go one step at a time, stop and give yourself a break, then continue to move forward.

Order

Order is a very delicate area. We must discipline and organize our day-to-day lives in a certain order:

Short-Term Goals
Long-Term Goals

Within each group, apply the following system:

Priority One
Priority Two (and so on)

The trick is to use common sense, logic, realistic tools and our feelings together before assigning the priority plan. When it is all done and clear, we need to ask the following questions:

- Why? This is the reason we need to juggle priorities.

- Where does the plan go from there?

- How do your flexibility and changes impact the outcome?

  - We have so much in our control, and at the same time we have so little that we can control absolutely. Therefore when new events, other people's actions, weather, money situations, family emergencies and such things affect our plans, we need to learn how to juggle our priority list.

  - The most important task is not to lose sight of the plan. Be challenged, but be calm. Do not introduce ego battles, selfishness or temper tantrums. They will take you nowhere.

  - You must understand that change is a constant. This is a great aspect of our lives. Can you imagine how boring life would be if everything always remained the same? Yes, perhaps some people might prefer it that way, but most of us seek new experiences and excitement, and with every change and movement we grow tremendously. Experience is the richest tool of all. Time gives us that tool unconditionally.

- When we apply *discipline, organization* and *order* in our careers, this paints an altogether different picture.

- Then we have fewer factors to deal with.

- An action list can be prepared in consideration of deadlines and the priority schedule, but there will always be some room for changes, such as:

    - A visit from an unexpected customer.

    - The imported goods that did not arrive on time.

    - The shipment that got lost.

    - The customer who did not pay when the commitment was made.

    - Valuable machinery that broke down.

    - A key employee who called in sick.

    - Facing the facts, we must reorganize our priority schedule according to the company's needs, namely the flow of work and the finances involved. Ultimately we want to seek the best results overall for the operation and organization of the company.

    - Most of the time we are not emotional when crises occur at work, but we can be completely out of control when personal, emotional crises arise. Then we lose the fruitfulness of time in the process of solving the problem.

That is where I assign the factor of *destination*. This is what I mean:

- For most of our lives we concentrate on the destination, the result, the outcome and the end product of our efforts.

- We need to reach and achieve a level of success as we see fit.

- We must purchase certain material items, and we look forward to the moment when we will have them and own them.

Destinations

So what happens between destinations? How do we utilize the time between those stations? Where does it go? Do we enjoy the time between point A and point B? Or are we always in the driver's seat, never stopping to see the path that leads to the goal or the place or the relationship? This is an area of great importance, so let me be more specific. For example:

George is a highly regarded corporate executive. He has it all—a wonderful wife, two beautiful children, a large home in a good area, a sports car and stylish clothes. He is physically fit, looks great and has a charming personality.

He is in charge of negotiating large contracts for a distribution company. George needs to travel abroad at least five times a year. He prefers first class and eats in the best restaurants at home as well as during his travels. He has a quality support staff that reports directly to him.

It would seem that George has everything. Wouldn't anyone like to be in his place, collecting his large salary, plus the bonuses and company stock? He is set for life. But there are a few areas we should not forget to question.

Does George get enough sleep? Does he spend enough time with his family? Does he know how to enjoy a simple afternoon smelling the roses in his backyard? Does he walk over to the ice cream parlor and enjoy a leisurely treat during a hot summer evening? Does he have enough time to read about new inventions, innovative products on the market, the travel section of his local paper? Does he smile often? Is he completely fulfilled and content? Or is he always looking forward to his next purchase, such as a home, a boat or a car? When did he have his last checkup? Is he really in perfect shape?

No, he is stressed. He feels overwhelmed at times. He gets very little sleep. He spends only a few hours a week with his family. He works late when he is in town, or he has late business meetings and eats out without the family. He is always in a hurry. He focuses on the next project without finishing the one he is working on. His financial commitments are higher and higher every year. He is anxious and has very little patience for his kids when he comes home after a long day at work. He forgets to be more affectionate with his wife. Sex has become less and less important to him. And George is only thirty-seven years old.

So what is happening with his time between destinations? He experiences a huge void, a clear space with nothing to fill it.

Here are the valuable points to learn about the time between our destinations.

Filling the Time Between Business Destinations:

- Take mini-breaks throughout the time assigned to accomplish your destination.

- Detach yourself mentally from the project.

- Refuel your mind by taking a short walk, reading a fun magazine, listening to a happy tune, playing an instrument, breathing slowly, looking at your childhood photo album, going for a drive, thinking of a movie you saw the day before, exploring your office building, smelling the freshly-trimmed grass and the planted flowers. Go and get a cup of coffee at Starbucks or some other coffee shop, instead of pouring yourself a quick cup of stale coffee in the cafeteria or the office kitchen.

- Stretch out—search the Web for a new tie, flowers for your partner, a small toy for the kids, a book, a tennis racket, a ball or a simple game.

- Build enthusiasm for your next short getaway. Perhaps it could be a fishing trip with your best friend.

- Pick up the phone and call your friend or favorite family member. Ask how they are doing. When will you see them again? What are they up to? Do they need help with anything? Ask if they have something new to share with you. Be interested and involved.

- Find a charity organization where you can be supportive to others.

- Stimulate your mind with something that is new and exciting for you, like joining a dance class or taking music lessons.

- Separate yourself from your work. Draw away and detach yourself to a point of release with something different—trivia, uplifting thoughts or listening to other voices besides yours.

By incorporating some of these diversions, you refuel your energy level, and the next task will seem easier and more productive. Teach yourself how to pro-act instead of reacting to everything that does not feel right for you or does not suit your expectations. It can be done!

In Your Personal Life, Between Destinations

- At home, do not always seek the next thing to do. Do you open your mail quickly, eat your dinner in a rush, take a hurried shower and run through time as fast as you can?

- Slow the process down.

- Yes, you have chores to do, but sort them out, using common sense and your free time to do so.

- In between the chores, take small breaks.

- Turn on the radio. By the second week, you'll be able to go outside and listen to the music you desire.

- Eat your meals slowly, and build a conversation with your loved ones between bites.

- If you are alone, enjoy and savor every bite of food. While you are eating, glance through a sports magazine, a travel magazine or a home decorating magazine.

- Take time out for a walk around your home.

- Stop and say hello to your next-door neighbor for a few minutes.

- Instead of driving, walk over to the grocery store or the pizza place, and walk back home.

- Go to the gym. Even 15 minutes is better than nothing.

- Open up your clothes closet and decide which clothes you can give away or get rid of.

- Keep less clutter in your home.

- Water the plants.

- Record your favorite show when you are away from home.

- Be more passionate with your partner.

- Spend more quality time with your kids, without watching TV or playing with toys. Talk to them and listen to them. Ask questions and be tuned in to their voices.

- Plan a social event.

- Invite friends or family for dinner.

- Cook your favorite dish. If you do not know how, purchase a cookbook that will teach you step-by-step.

- Physical work is good for you, especially when your career involves mostly mental work.

This is what is called *time between destinations*. Use it wisely and with enthusiasm. We almost always have time between the stations of our destinations. Time should be respected, appreciated and utilized with common sense and feelings. Time is there for you. What you do with it is entirely up to you. When you frequently use the phrase, "I don't have enough time to do this and that," what does it mean? It is the result of three facts:

- You do not know how to apply order, organization or discipline in your life.

- You do not understand the concept of time between destinations.

- You believe that you are doing your best, according to the lifestyle to which you are accustomed.

When you apply the segments I addressed earlier, you will be amazed to discover that you can stretch time, produce more with time and fill more time. The key is understanding how to enjoy the time between destinations.

All of the above does not mean that we should not have goals, be motivated, desire things or dream big. We should reach as high as we can. This is what life is all about. We can choose to live it fully and feel content and refreshed with every step we take.

When we concentrate only on the destination, the end result, the purpose, the mission, the greed, the power, the ego, the control and the money, we lose a sense of the richness of the time in between.

Time gives us everything we reach out for. Without time we have absolutely nothing. This fact must register clearly in our minds. We need to look at the clocks ticking around us as reminders of the time we do have. I do not mean to address this with a negative or pessimistic view. On the contrary, it is my delight. This is the light we must turn on in order to see clearly and acknowledge that time is here. We have the freedom and the wisdom to choose how to use it. Why? And where or in what fashion or style can we furnish and apply time to our advantage in our day-to-day lives, creating the results we seek?

Time does not dictate. Time is vibrating, and we can learn how and why to move forward with time and live in the moment—in the now—to expand time. Why not make the best of it?

Start now!

The Ancient Wisdom of Hats

Now, for the great finale of this formula, let's go back to the eighteenth century.

1. Hats were designed and worn as one of the most important garments at that time. Each hat was fitted to the status of the person who wore it by the form and shape of its design.

2. The color of the hat differentiated the financial status or power of the individual, including wealth, ancestry and position of leadership.

3. The way hats were worn also indicated the wearer's personal commitments.

4. The fabric of the hat separated the seasons.

5. The size of the hat indicated the gender of the wearer.

6. The movements of the hat were exercised according to the type of event: personal, intimate gathering, dispute, negotiation, business meeting, family get-together, the showing of respect and validating one's emotional status.

Here are some of the "rules" of hat etiquette:

Taking off the hat was a sign of respect and recognition. One would take off his hat upon entering any home, place of business or place of negotiations. Putting the hat back on the head was a symbol of walking out of a meeting, closure or a simple good-bye. Upon entering a place of humility or prayer or the office of a recognized leader, the hat had to be removed quickly and always held in the right hand. When entering a home, the wearer would remove his hat instantly and place it in a safe, protected place by the entrance, preferably next to the area for coats and other accessories in the wintertime such as gloves, scarves and boots.

Kings and queens wore elevated hats with jewels or precious stones. Their hats were usually dark purple, decorated with many amethysts and dark-blue sapphires. On very special occasions, royalty would wear crowns made of gold or silver layered with diamonds and precious stones. Their brilliance could be seen from a distance. A regal young girl would wear a hat with lace around it, a symbol of purity, innocence and availability. On special occasions, royalty wore pearl crowns with ruby-red stones or amethysts, usually with a round, dark-blue sapphire. On average days, royalty would wear medium-sized hats made of the finest silks, decorated with multiple colored stones and small diamonds.

A poor man or woman wore simple, dark, stiff wool hats. The poor would also turn down the brim to cover the forehead and hide the face. It was a sign of weakness, insecurity, cowardice and complete humility.

The businessman wore a large-brim hat with a sharp, pointed front. This meant that he was smart and well-respected. A young lady in search of a man wore a colorful hat, usually purple or blue, thinly tailored in the back. A prominent married woman wore a round, full hat, usually black, brown, gray or burgundy. The hat represented the existence of the partnership and security. Children wore thin little hats, designed in a nearly square shape, for protection and to symbolize the learning that was ahead of them.

Teachers wore black hats as a symbol of authority, academic knowledge and supervision. The position was taken seriously. People in the medical field wore dark-green hats, a pleasing color to the eye. They believed that green was the most pleasant color to observe, because it matched the color of the outside greenery. Artists and musicians would wear dark-blue and dark-purple hats made of shiny materials like silk or satin, with a very thin brim. They stood out in crowds.

Gypsies and very poor people wore only black, very flat hats. They were made of thick, rough wool and fit their heads completely, showing no brim at all.

Country people in the small towns wore a light-brown hat made of straw or leaves for the summer season. The hat was round and large to protect them from the sun. In the wintertime, they wore small hats made of sheepskin, with flaps that covered their cheeks and ears and tied together under the chin to warm their faces during the brutally cold days and nights.

Dancers or common girls ready to be with anyone wore a bright-red hat with lots of colorful silk or shiny ribbons tied around the neck. They were treated poorly and disrespectfully. The tie meant that they could be bought with goods or money.

Priests wore small hats on top of their heads, mostly of red, thick wool, gathered in the middle of the hat and pointed. The height of the hat reminded the crowd that they were centered, together and spiritually wise, with their thoughts guided by God. Such hats also symbolized that priests were extremely powerful and influential. The fabric gathered in the middle of the hat also separated them from the rest of the people. They were on a higher level, and they ruled with fear, judgment and endless expectations.

Revolutionary or influential people wore gray hats with a wide black trim. The hats were thin and small, indicating the sharpness of their leadership, creating a narrow bridge of followers at all costs. They were made with a small, thin cap in the front and completely flat in the back. Athletic individuals wore the same type of hats in various colors such as blue, brown, black and rust.

Indeed, hats meant something in those days.

a. Hats had something to say.

b. Hats represented title and status.

c. Hats were created for fashion and clarity.

d. Hats had to fit the time, place and purpose of the message.

e. Hats were meaningful.

f. Hats were treated seriously and with great respect.

g. Hats were a significant part of the clothing of the day; everyone wore them.

h. Changing the position of the hat had a purpose. As a point of contemporary reference, this would be analogous to graduates moving their tassels from one side of the mortarboard to the other.

Now let me share with you the connection between what was once called "The Ancient Wisdom of Hats" and today's "Time—Life—Love—Time Original Formula," while I incorporate destination, order, organization, discipline and the wisdom of living in the now. Not only will you understand the formula, you will also enjoy and apply it in a playful fashion, releasing stress along the way and practicing it completely on your own. You will walk away with a tool to last you a lifetime.

That is why I titled it the "Time—Life—Love—Time Original Formula."

Let me help you with the concept of wearing the mental hat. I will design the following hats for you by color, shape, fabric and trimmings. Hats are in and vintage is cool! So let's open with some specific colors.

White

The white hat is made of fine silk and completely round. Wear it at home—a peaceful place you want to keep that way. Focus only on your home life and detach yourself from everything else, especially the outside world.

Red

The red hat is made of a thick ribbon silk, high and round in the front and square in the back. Wear the red hat when you are out having fun with friends or lovers, especially for dinner, a movie, walks together, storytelling time and other forms of entertainment. Red indicates passion, a break from the routine. You have lots of exuberance when you socialize. Be entertaining, be fun, be light and energetic. People generally love to be around energetic, fun and charismatic personalities. Detach yourself from responsibilities, worries, work, finances and personal matters that trouble you. Enjoy every second of your time wearing this hat.

Purple

The purple hat is very sheer; it represents the clarity you are seeking, an understanding of who you are, your why, your destination. Wear this hat when you are in a meditation mode, seeking intimate time with yourself. Wear it during quiet times when you exclude everyone else, when you are one with yourself, not lonely but free of doubts, fears, concerns, work and other duties. You need to detach yourself completely and stay put. Do this exercise three to four times a week, for ten to fifteen minutes on each of these days. The purple hat is a powerful yet calming color. It gives you the desire and the strength to separate yourself from the outside world, focusing on you. You may choose to wear it at the park, on the beach, in the mountains or even in the desert to keep you centered. Be in the now.

Dark Green

The green hat is made of a thick wool, showing financial strength and wisdom. Wear the deep dark-green hat when you are dealing with business or work. It is appropriate for a business owner, a shop owner or all types of workers. Dark green represents the color of currency, abundance and the approach toward and respect for money. It also represents appreciation given to the customer. It shows that you put a great deal of thinking into the products you sell or represent. Focus on the business and be proactive when necessary. Understand your business or your work and be open to learn. Dark green also manifests experience, stability and hope.

Blue

Wear the blue hat when you exercise, walk, swim, sail, ski or participate in any other athletic activity. Blue is the color of the sky and the ocean. The ocean is always changing. It is moving and flowing. It is endless and spectacular. Do not look at the winning moment. Let your own journey move and flow; treat it with endless enthusiasm. You can change within the game. Flow with it and the results will be rewarding. Blue also has a calming effect on us. Be centered, be calm and do not feel anxious.

Wear the light blue hat when you drive a vehicle: a car, truck, boat or airplane. Blue is leadership in motion. Waters and rivers are in constant motion. Blue is the color of the sky on a clear day. We need to see the direction we take.

Black

Wear the black hat only as a sign of respect for others in their difficult moments. As soon as you give your respect, take it off and replace it with the light-blue one, which means that you are again in the driver's seat, controlling your life humbly, without an ego, and recognizing the difference.

Yellow

The yellow hat is for parents. As a parent, you need to exercise your utmost knowledge and experience in dealing with your children. They need your guidance and expertise. They ask for discipline in so many ways. Parents need to listen to the words between the lines and understand how kids react to voices, harsh words, punishment, impatience, arguments at home, loneliness and the lack of joy for life. Kids are influenced tremendously by the parents' behavior and approach to stress, challenge and money situations. Social circles will also influence your children's life as well as their choice of partners, the home built for them and the environment at home. Yellow is for sunshine and warmth. As a parent, you need to bring these into your children's upbringing and their growth within the process. Yellow is also the color of the moon. It lights up your heart and your being. When you become a parent, your heart gets that special light. Maintain it throughout your entire life. Once a parent, always a parent, regardless of your own age or the age of your children.

Brown

Wear the brown hat when you are facing a stressful situation. You must be realistic when wearing this hat. Brown is the color of the leaves in the fall. They are not strong. The leaves fall on the ground. The brown hat is a reminder of vulnerability. It represents the choice we need to make, not to react but to pro-act, in a stressful situation. It also validates the other person's needs and moments of weakness. You too can fall down when your ego is leading you instead of humility. Let control go, and the situation will become more under control. Brown is in-between black and other colors. You can choose the space between and leave the situation on hold for a while. Address challenges when the proper time comes, just like picking up a leaf and placing it in your favorite book as a precious bookmark.

Pink

Wear the pink hat when you are getting together with family members. Pink is a peaceful, pleasant color. It will reflect your behavior and your approach to getting together with family. So often people bring the wrong energy. Family members may have no chemistry between them. Some love to get into confrontations and arguments. Some love to compete and talk only about themselves, letting their egos run the show. At times family members may not feel close to one another and bring out their worst characteristics. By wearing the pink hat, you keep a certain peace when you get together. You feel uplifted, and you do not react to other family members' behavior by placing more wood on the fire. You are content and you keep on smiling. As we all know, we cannot change others' moods or personalities. Family get-togethers are very important and vital in keeping your own household together. Everyone can bear a few hours around relatives with whom they do not have the best connections. It's okay. The pink hat also represents short-term togetherness. The relatives will go home eventually, or you will leave, returning to your own life.

Wearing pink will also teach you how to introduce more humor to the occasion—jokes, laughter and light, trivial conversation. When we bring that type of approach and behave calmly and pleasantly, we impact the rest of the family. If they came initially with bitterness, anger, jealousy and negative thoughts, the laughter and the jokes will diminish their power and influence. For some people this is easier than for others. They can behave diplomatically and respectfully, controlling how they feel about those family members. However, when the situation is not pleasant, that is the time to remind yourself that you are wearing the pink hat and that the situation is only temporary. The pink hat will bring out the best in you, and you will walk away much less stressed and bothered. Social events and family gatherings are supposed to be enjoyable. You should not have to work too hard to make them pleasant, and time will pass by faster that way. It works every time for me, and believe me, every family has some people you would rather not see at all. You can choose friends, but you cannot choose to belong to another family. You were born into one family, while new members were added through marriages, daughters-in-law, sons-in-law, brothers-and sisters-in-law, parents-in-law, cousins, stepchildren and adoptions. Still, we can choose to be on our best behavior and play the game just right.

Multicolored

Wear your multicolored hat when you are on vacation. A good mix of colors would be blue, green, red and yellow. The multicolored hat is the symbol of being open-minded. Invite your vacation place into your album of experiences. Become familiar with the place. Enjoy every second of it. You are on vacation. Be completely there mentally and physically. Stay in the moment. Walk around the area; watch, listen and see the differences between the place where you live and the vacation spot. Greet people with a smile. Do not be too bashful to ask questions if you get lost or come across a place that is quite interesting and you want to know more about it. Sometimes we bond quickly with a new place, and sometimes it takes us several days to be comfortable there. Certain people hardly ever feel right in a new place. They imagined it, they planned on it, but when they got there it seemed too foreign and too far from their expectations. What do you do then? You remind yourself that you are wearing the multicolored hat. Slowly you adapt to the place, knowing that you are only there for a few days. You will be back home in no time. Time is moving forward. What do we understand by that? We need to do the same, but for now let go of your control and give yourself a chance to enjoy the experience. You are adding a bit more knowledge to your book of life. Isn't that worth something? You are enriching yourself with this visit. If the place does not look or feel or represent everything you saw in the brochure, make the best of it. Do not fight with your feelings and disappointments. Take it easy. You are there already. See and examine what else is out there. Pick and choose. The worst that can happen is that you will not go back there again.

If the food does not agree with you, try fruits, vegetables, bread and cheese. Eat what makes you feel right. Several times I went to a new place and thoroughly enjoyed myself, but the food was too foreign and did not agree with me completely. I went to the local grocery store and bought a few rolls, some butter, cheese, tomatoes, cucumbers, peppers, apples and grapes. I ate that way for several days. My stomach was never empty and I felt good. I wound up spending very little money on food.

You can make a new situation work out in your favor by being open-minded, concentrating on the practical side of the matter, using your common sense, and gaining experience from the adventure. When you visit a place with loved ones or go to see people you care about, your heart is filled with a loving connection. Give energy to that feeling and everything else is much less important. When you get home and flash back to the place you just left and develop your photographs, they bring to mind a sharp recollection and you say to yourself, "I've been there, I know how it is there, I got to see the place," and then you can go back to your regular routine. Vacation is supposed to be a colorful experience.

Peach/Orange

Wear a peach or orange hat when you shop. Think of an orange or a peach in nature. It is pleasant to the eye. It is inviting. Peach and orange are the colors of the sun. We need warmth and brightness for shopping. You are welcome in the store or shopping area. You feel good. You are about to spend some money for new things. It is a momentary satisfaction, especially when you see beautiful things for your home and become creative in your mind. You can see how that particular vase or chair will look in your living room. When you shop for clothes for yourself, you gain confidence and recognition by watching yourself in the mirror. You look good. It fits you perfectly. Shopping for gifts brings a sense of giving and appreciation. Automatically we feel uplifted and enthused. The peach color is a flag that warns us not to end up with a lemon when we go shopping. When you are out shopping for a bicycle, a motorcycle, a car, a boat or a house, do your homework and your study beforehand. Be intelligent and educate yourself. Take your time. Let time achieve your goals. Do not end up with a lemon of a purchase, because lemons can never be peaches. Bite into a peach. It will taste sweet and delightful to you. A lemon can be bitter and sour when you squeeze it into your mouth. Just look in the mirror and see the difference.

Gray

Wear the gray hat when you need to make a decision of any sort. Remember, a decision is not always black or white. Do not make the decision too quickly. For certain circumstances or moments, we need to wear the gray hat. We cannot be judgmental at such times. There is a fine line between extremes.

Let me give you an example. So many people out there are gifted, talented and highly intelligent. They learn about a particular topic for many years. They become very book-smart. They learn the technical part of the data, the research and the final outcome according to the literature on the subject.

Then they experience the reality of the situation. An architect, one of the best in his class, creates an incredible high-rise building out of paper and aluminum, using glue and other adhesives to hold it together. He has never worked in the outside world. Eventually this architect finds himself out in the job market. He receives an extraordinary offer, so he accepts. The very first project is a high-rise building in a big city next to the water. The weather there is very humid, and it rains continuously for four to six months of the year. The city has also experienced a few earthquakes in the past.

The architect soon learns that it is not all about the books he read or the sample projects he did. He has to take many other factors into consideration. So his design decisions are not truly black or white. You have to observe the in-between facts, and be flexible and open in order to read and understand the fine print in the gray areas.

A teacher cannot approach each student in the same way or expect the same kind of work from everyone. The students may be in the same class, but each one is different. All students are products of their families, backgrounds, social and economic situations, geographical locations and beliefs. They have their own perception of things. Students react in different ways to new information. They have their own personalities. The teacher or professor needs to place the gray area in front of them. Teachers must not be too structured or set in their ways. Teachers present the academic topic in one form, but they also have to add their own thoughts and observations about the material in order to specifically target the learning styles of individual students. Students cannot be classified as good or bad; many of them are somewhere between those extremes. They can be great one year, and with the impact of an emotional or personal event they can turn around and be the opposite the following year.

Gray represents clouds covering up clarity. It also teaches you how to appreciate and see clearly when the situation is resolved. Gray is the color of fog. When you are driving and it's getting very foggy out there and you cannot see where you're going, you need to drive carefully. The road can be dangerous. What do you do? You stop and wait patiently to allow some time for it to clear up. Then you can pursue your mission. Indeed, gray is the color of being alert, awake and cautious about time.

Navy

Wear a white hat with navy-blue stripes when you study or pray. Wear a navy-blue hat when you are conducting a meeting, speaking in front of an audience or presenting a product. This hat is also for lawyers in the courtroom. Navy is a friendly, businesslike and professional color. It suits the occasion in a very special fashion. It is not black and it is not a light color. Some also call it midnight blue, the color of the sky at night. Navy blue is an inviting color, yet serious and respected. It is a clean color, and every other color enhances it. It is very accommodating. White, powder-blue, green, yellow, pink, beige, brown, purple, wine and even black all look right with navy. Imagine the sky at night. The stars shine like diamonds, lighting up the sky. You can spot them so easily on a clear night. A business presentation, a meeting, a speaking engagement or a day in court must show the foundation and the teachings for clarity and results.

When you attend such a place, you hope to walk away with something, a tool in your hands to be utilized and practiced in the future. You will place your own stars as your achievements are accomplished one by one.

Light Green (with blue in it)

Wear a light-green hat with white stripes when you deal with patients. This is primarily for doctors, nurses, surgeons, assistants, therapists, clinics, hospitals and medical office staffs. Light green is such a significant color in nature: green grass, green leaves, green plums, green almonds, green apples, green cucumbers, green peppers and so much more. Green is a color of comfort. Green is calm and soothing. Green is so pleasant to the eye. Green is also the color of the ocean from far away.

An individual working in the medical field needs to be calm and bright, filled with ideas and solutions to health problems. A patient looking at the so-called :"medically-powered" individual becomes less anxious and less emotional and possesses the ability to listen clearly to the message delivered. The appearance of the color green brings them closer to reality, and it can and does ease the pain. I am not referring to physical pain. I mean the inner, emotional, mental kind of pain. The color green also gives patients the strength to be more practical and understanding. Light green is very natural and trusting. It feels right and it looks right. You can also wear green when you address someone who has no experience. Green is a fresh start in all areas of our lives.

Lavender

Wear a lavender hat when you dance, sing, listen to music or just move to the rhythm. Lavender is full of nostalgia. You embrace art. You express art. Your share your feelings through art. Art brings out emotions, talents and skills you never thought you had. Your creative side is flowing. You are detaching yourself from responsibilities and the work plan. Art takes you to a fun place. Art is therapy. It is not an escape. Art is the break between chores, between financial concerns, schedules, organization and order.

Be an Original!

Wear a hat with multiple dots (such as a background of red with large purple dots and little yellow dots) when you are making love. With multiple dots on your head? Whoa! It sounds funny and eccentric. Your initial thought will be, *No hats when you make love! It is taboo!* Well, not really. Have you ever found a rule prohibiting it? Making love is an art. Making love and being in love mean getting out of your shell. You give yourself all the way and you do not hold back. You are completely in the moment, detaching yourself from everything else. You are flowing and you are on a high. It is the most unique high you can feel. When you make love, you see the stars, the colors of the rainbow and the sunlight coming into your body and soul at the same time.

Making love is special when it is not only a physical act. It can be very empty that way for either women or men. When individuals seek only physical satisfaction, they walk away with a certain emptiness, or at times with a feeling of victory. One more conquest. "I had the chance to be with him/her and now I am free. I can go on to the next one." What happens then? You repeat the pattern. You move on to the next one and yet another one, but you go home alone and you stay home alone.

It is true that at times we must live alone or be alone to get to know ourselves—who we are and where we are going after or in between experiences. However, making love is the finest connection and bonding possible between two people.

I can compare it to something very simple and you will understand. Here is the experiment. Take a clear glass and pour into it only one drop of water or juice or other liquid. Let your partner pour in another drop of the same liquid. What happens? The two drops become one and you cannot separate them. That is what lovemaking can be all about. Two together become one in every possible way. They cannot be separated by thoughts, actions or ideas.

They are completely bonded and the time is speckled with dots, the symbols of the various feelings you are reaching and releasing at the same time. In reality, considering everything else that we do, we spend very little time making love. I am not referring simply to sex. So why not make it precious, special and unique? It is supposed to take you away from everything and allow you to be in the moment. The dots stand for the thin line between your background, your existence, your life and the main game you play.

Making love can always be a winning game for both parties. Be considerate, be there for one another, and pick the right time, when you can truly be in dots and not in doubt. Do not fear making love. When we use the words "make love," we understand that we are talking about making a work of art together and that the piece is perfect. Do not hold back. After making love you not only feel refueled, relaxed and at ease, you are in a complete state of detachment from stress.

Exercise, proper diet, lots of sleep, vacation time, money and so on are very important tools for adding quality to our lives and making them better and longer. Making love is all of the above in one drop. It is powerful. It is natural. It is complete giving and receiving. One needs to learn the skill of receiving; when you do, you know how and when to give. Time will be there for you. Just make time for the experience.

◆   ◆   ◆

We spoke earlier about art. I want to add that it is so important for kids to be exposed to art in their formative years and to pursue their talents. Art is a healthy hobby. We excel when we become passionate. Art is passion. Art is exuberance, and art can make us so enthusiastic and free.

a. When you develop a talent in art, you become more humble. You release some of your ego and feel more depth in your soul.

b. Feelings—what is life without them?

c. A poet feels a moment of passion, and is eager to share it by capturing the same feeling when he writes the poem.

d. A painter expresses so much of his feelings, experiences and true perceptions of a person or place or animal that is the subject of his picture.

e. Some artists prefer abstraction. Look at the colors they use. These reflect their mood and outlook on life.

f. The beauty of art is that you can translate feelings and invite them into your life in whatever shape, form, color or interpretation you choose.

g. Each and every one of us can look at a painting and perceive it differently.

The freedom of choice, the freedom of time and the freedom of feeling—this is how art makes us grow. Blessed are the people who can be very practical, realistic, intelligent, well-organized, and at the same time extremely creative and artistic. They have all the tools to build an incredible life for themselves and the people around them. They color life with common sense, and their time is used wisely and joyfully.

Most people are either practical or artistic. But we can modify that by introducing more art and freedom of expression in various shapes and forms when children begin to attend school. I believe that everyone is special. Every person has some talent or skill they can develop.

• As you learn about time, organization, order, discipline and come to an understanding of destinations, you validate your feelings. Each and every one of you can produce good results, especially if you are an individual with a high level of creativity and individualistic behavior.

- Remember, the choices you make cannot always be black or white. You need to find and address in in-betweens, the fine line that separates us from emotions, reality, the desire to live fully and the excitement of life, regardless of the challenges we must face along the way.

How many times have you gotten lost or missed the exit?

- Wear your blue hat—be in control.

- Study and know where you are going ahead of time.

- If you're sad, your road is becoming cloudy or turning dark. You need to regroup in order to be in control again.

- Others depend on you. This cannot be taken lightly. After all, you are leading them.

- Blue is the traditional color we use for boys more often than for girls, but today anything goes.

- Blue also stands for physical work. Physical work is very good for you. If you need to fix the vehicle, you are a contributor.

Can you imagine life without the sky? Without water? We need people out there to mend things, drive vehicles and lead us where we need to go. Not everyone can or should be a scholar. Take the driver's seat and let time make it happen for you.

When you sleep, wear no hat at all—you are in the rest mode. You peel off all your titles and labels. You take off the hats, and you are completely free and clear of everything.

Time is the precious tool you need to live. With it, you can accomplish everything you dream and desire. Without it, there is nothing. Remember:

- You need to take this time for you.

- It is exclusively yours.

- You should not think of anything.

- You should not worry about anything.

- You have to be still.

- You are stepping away from and out of your living mode.

- When you wake up, you start a new day as if you had a new life.

- You are grateful and thankful for the new chance.

- Life is as fresh as a child's breath with the scent of a young white rose, with the taste of honey and the feeling of total love in your heart and soul.

- You've got time all over again.

I have developed a love affair with time, and the relationship is growing stronger and deeper as time moves forward. I keep up with a big smile, and you can too!

Join me in the circle of time.

◆   ◆   ◆

Please understand that you have the choice to wear or use the imaginary hats for all purposes. They exist to help you switch from role to role in your daily life. We cannot deal with everything we face in life in the same fashion, color, shape, tone of voice or attitude.

Most importantly, you need to learn to switch these imaginary hats on and off to release stress and detach from the clutter in your life. Focus on the now—the role you are assuming at this very moment—and be the best at it that you can be. You will succeed and excel, because you are giving and devoting your best quality time to it.

How do you learn to utilize time wisely, moving from emotional behavior into reality, always searching for true facts and positive results? Only by living in the now and blocking out all the other interruptions and disturbances around us. We cannot handle everything at once and solve all our problems at the same time. Challenges will come and go, but change it always certain.

By practicing the formula with the "Ancient Wisdom of Hats," playfully choosing which colors, shapes and textures to imagine, you will reach the point where you, too, love time.

You need to keep switching, peeling off and putting on your various hats to remind yourself of the places you go and the roles you play in your daily life. You will fulfill your expectations and your enthusiasm. Keep all of your hats clean. This could be the most important piece of clothing you wear. Build your own boxes to store them safely; they cannot be folded. They need to stand out, and so do you.

By wearing the hats and detaching yourself every single time from the outer circle, you can maintain a clear channel within that enables you to stay in the moment. The results will be amazing. You will reduce your stress levels because you are dealing with one thing at a time. So get out there and detach your-self from the next project, the next meeting and whatever else is preventing you from living in the now.

The various hats represent various relationships with time, the moments you take in life to achieve an individual fit. You wear multiple titles and roles within your life, but you can become rich with wisdom and experience when you apply and practice this very simple program. You can smile more often and be fulfilled.

Understand and accept changes, the highs and the lows of life, in their proper fashion. Do you remember the sale mentioned earlier? Life will always present this sale.

The Last Hat

I have left one hat for last. When we feel beautiful, we want to look attractive. We put on our favorite clothes, shoes and accessories. At the same time we will wear a clear, see-through hat with light-blue dots. The hat is clear so that we can see through the entire exterior. We show the inner us—our true character. Let us shine from within. We must be clear at all times with our direction and purpose.

The light-blue dots represent the challenge, the scale between the good and the evil, the temptation. The concentration on material things, on looks, has become an important factor in our modern lives. Yet we fail to accept one important fact. These things do not last. They may keep you going for a while, but they cannot lift you and give you all the strength you need at difficult moments.

See clearly and keep a sharp mind. Be strong. Turn on the switch and find the light within the commotion of your life's events. Enjoy the now. Be good to yourself. Acknowledge the importance of others. Understand the reason for relationships and your time alone, the time between destinations, your goals and your achievement of the mark.

Value time. Cherish it and love it. You have the freedom to do whatever you want with it. Life is time, and time fills life. Love time and enjoy your life! Live in the now! Be a true friend to stress, deal with it in the now, and move forward with your life.

Thank you for sharing your special time with me.

May I share a short story with you?

A few years back, the corporation I was working for as a franchise relationship executive invited the management staff to a cruise on a lovely boat. It was in the middle of the summer, and the boat was cruising around the San Pedro Harbor and back to Marina del Rey.

We had a few refreshing drinks and a huge ice cream cake for dessert. It was a fun social time, and everyone was in a great mood, laughing and talking and listening to the music the deejay played.

I was standing on the balcony, when I noticed a large yacht cruising by us. Two young girls sat suntanning on the deck. They were already cocoa-colored, and their white bathing suits contrasted dramatically with their skin.

The boat sped off, and the foamy ocean waves cleared a powerful path to follow. That was when I noticed the large gold letters engraved on the back of the yacht. They spelled: WHAT'S NEXT?

It made me think. We entertain our minds continuously, toying with thoughts of what is next. And indeed, what is next may be sweet, exciting and fruitful. In the meantime, however, we can be fulfilled with the now, extracting priceless wisdom from it.

Use your common-sense tools. Time will turn what's next into the now for you.

There are a few more important areas I should mention, such as behavior patterns and research work, anger management and negative energy, and other related topics. All of these are connected with time and time management. When you apply the formula wisely, you will encounter fewer difficulties and problems in dealing with these issues, so the connections are extremely significant.

I would like to take this opportunity to share some references and quotes I have gathered for you. I believe they will prove to be of great value:

Karen Leland is the coauthor of the recent book *Watercolor Wisdom: How Smart People Prosper in the Face of Conflict, Pressure, and Change*. The book is based on surveys of over 20,000 people around the world. *Ladies Home Journal, Time, Newsweek, Woman's Day,* CBS, CNN, NBC, Oprah and many others have interviewed Karen.

Carol Kauffman, PhD, ABPP, is an Assistant Clinical Professor at Harvard Medical School and an expert in emotional intelligence and positive psychology coaching. She writes: "People do not understand how to harness emotions for optimal performance. Often, emotions become obstacles instead. The challenge is to know WHEN emotions (time) are fact or fiction. As fact they are important 'data.' As fiction they are illusions that can compel us to do what is not in our best interest."

Stephen Shapiro writes about emotional behavior in his latest book, *Goal-Free Living: How to Have the Life You Want Now* (Wiley). This volume is all about focusing on the now. He shares eight secrets of being more goal-free and more present-oriented:

- Use a compass, not a map. Have a sense of direction (not a specific destination) and then meander with purpose.

- Trust that you are never lost. Every seemingly wrong turn is an opportunity to learn and experience new things.

- Remember that opportunity knocks often but sometimes softly. While we blindly pursue goals, we often miss unexpected and wonderful possibilities.

- Want what you have. Measure your life by your yardstick and appreciate who you are, what you do and what you have now.

- Seek out adventure. Treat your life as a one-time-only journey and revel in the new and different.

- Become a people-magnet. Constantly attract, build and nurture relationships with new people so that you always have the support and camaraderie of others.

- Embrace your limits. Transform your inadequacies and boundaries into unique qualities that you can use to your advantage.

- Remain detached. Focus on the present, act with a commitment to the future, and avoid worrying about how things will turn out.

During a 15-year tenure with the international consulting firm Accentor, Stephen established and led the Global Process Excellence Practice and developed innovation training that was delivered to 20,000 consultants. In 2001 he wrote the book *24/7 Innovation* (McGraw Hill), which has been featured in *Investor's Business Daily* and *The New York Times*. *Goal-Free Living* became number one on amazon.com's "Business Motivation" list and the number one "Self Improvement" bestseller on barnbesandnoble.com. It was also featured in *Entrepreneur Magazine* and was the cover story in *O: The Oprah Magazine*. Stephen has advised many leading organizations, including Staples, GE, Fidelity Investments, BMW Williams F1, Frito-Lay, UPS and Bristol-Myers Squibb.

Lisa McLoed is an author and speaker who has been featured on *Good Morning America* and in *The New York Times*, *Guideposts Magazine, Real Simple, Time* and *O: The Oprah Magazine*. Her book *Forget Perfect* (Penguin/Putnam) is hilarious help for all those who have ever put themselves last on their own priority list.

She claims that while working in the entertainment media industry, she came to a realization that "people in creative fields are more prone to fly off the handle." Whereas accountants and other traditional business types are skilled at stuffing their emotions (resulting in ulcers and heart attacks), people in creative, more relationship-driven fields have to tap into their emotions daily, so they are much closer to the surface, including the nasty ones. The reason people get angry quickly is that the anger is constantly bubbling under the surface before the "trigger" incident ignites it.

"Are angry people driven by negative energy?" she asks. "Yes, and at the root of their anger is fear, which is the negative emotion that fuels the quick reactions and irrational outbursts."

She also asks, "How do you separate emotions from practical solutions?" (This is what I refer to as pro-act instead of react. The proper time to make choices and decisions is when you are at the in-between destinations.) "Believe it or not, ignoring the emotions only makes it worse. The best way to move through it is not to respond with your own emotions, but to call them on the carpet by naming and acknowledging theirs."

Lisa quotes an example: "Irv, you seem so angry. I think that a vein in your head is about to pop. What is bothering you? And how can we get through these emotions so we can get back to work?"

Anger depends on more anger to fuel it, just like a two-year-old whose tantrum subsides when the parent calmly says, "I know you are angry because you want the Skittles, but all the fist-pounding in the world is not going to make me change my mind."

Jack Mayer, a Professor of Psychology at the University of New Hampshire, quotes the following question, written to him by Lori Wright of Media Relations at the University, and his answer.

"Is your personality making you sick?"

"Could be. Personality plays a critical part in a person's health. Hostile people are more susceptible to heart disease, and those who do not handle stress well are more apt to contract viral infections such as colds. Untold secrets harm health; sharing the secrets (in the right context) can reduce visits to the doctor. Conscientiousness also matters. Following your doctor's public health advice (assuming the advice is good) promotes longevity."

Mayer has developed a new way of understanding personality, which he describes in his book *Personality: A Systems Approach.*

"Personality is the master system of a person's psychological life, including motives and emotions, knowledge and intelligence, social skills and actions, and self-awareness and control.

"Much of our mental, psychological life carries on automatically. We get up in the morning, go to work or school, have conversations and the like, often without much self-reflection. Sometimes, though, things go wrong, or things go right, but they do not go right enough.

"Fortunately for us, we are endowed with a part of personality—that area of conscious management, including self-awareness and control, that allows us to stop, pause, and figure out what went wrong or what could go better. To do this, we have to understand a bit about our own personality—our own needs, our feelings, our mental capacities and social skills—and how those qualities fit into the world."

It is possible to change your personality, but often it is not easy. Personality is a "slow to express, slow to change system"— and after we decide some aspect of our personality is worth changing, it will take some persistence to actually accomplish it.

Anna Maravelas is president of TheraRising, Inc., an organization that focuses on conflict resolution and stress management in the workplace. Anna's strategies have appeared in more than 15 publications, including *The New York Times, Harvard Management Update* and *The American Bar Association Journal.* She is the author of *How to Reduce Workplace Conflict or Stress* (Career Press, 2005).

Anna also created a popular workplace seminar entitled "Self-Defeating Habits of Otherwise Brilliant People." During this seminar, corporate leaders learn how to avoid "emotional stupidity" by managing their reactions to frustrations. The leaders identify how they get "duped by the dazzle of contempt" and demonstrate 12 self-defeating costs of indignation, blame and backstabbing.

Anna writes, "Frustration is the most common trigger of workplace anger, stress and hostility. We experience 30 frustrations, heart hassles or mini-crises a day. That results in more than 750,000 in our lifetime."

People who aren't conscious of how they're responding to aggravations become increasingly annoyed or impatient as the day unfolds. Every hostile (either "hot" or "cold" hostility) response to frustration results in a chemical shift that lingers for two hours. A poorly-handled frustration in the morning physiologically sets people up for increasingly negative reactions as the day unfolds.

Anger and hostility are called "flooding" in medical and biofeedback studies. Flooding is a rapid release of hormones, adrenaline and cortisol in response to a physical threat or inflammatory thinking (i.e., "I can't stand this! Sales always screws up these orders!"). Blood pressure and heart rate increase. The blood thickens and the risk of arteriosclerosis increases.

Flooding is a silent killer and highly related to heart disease. In a study at Duke University, the death rate for highly hostile men in their mid-40s was four times that of men with low hostility rates. Chronic anger is a significant risk, not only for heart disease but sudden death, back pain and headaches.

When we become angry, we shift from the cortex, the problem-solving engine of the brain, to the medulla, the fight-or-flight center, which is about the size of a walnut and located at the base of the skull.

Biofeedback studies have shown that once the heartbeat exceeds 100, we cannot hear what the other person is saying even if we try.

Flooding results in feelings of severe emotional stress.

The following technique addresses the root cause of hostility. It takes into account the uphill physiological battle people face when trying to regain control, and the loss of IQ that hostile people experience (or what I call "emotional stupidity").

Calming a "Flooded" Employee or Customer: EASE

- Empathize. Empathy is a stated understanding of how the other person feels. It helps us connect with and therefore calm the other person. People escalate because they do not feel heard or understood. If you put yourself in their shoes and adopt their perspective, you'll quickly feel empathy for their frustrations (and, most likely, feelings that they've been treated with disrespect). This understanding of their position is extremely soothing.

- Appreciate. Expressing genuine appreciation for someone diminishes his or her hostility. People drop their hostility in a heartbeat in order to be appreciated by another person. (Remember, flooding results in feelings of severe emotional stress.) If you cannot make a genuine statement of appreciation for the person's commitment or skill, make a statement about their investment in solving the problem and eliminating unnecessary snafus.

- Speculate. Most people flood because of inflammatory thinking (see above), not the event itself. They assume that their frustration is the result of someone else's callousness or stupidity. Help them regain their problem-solving capacity (shift back to the cortex) by speculating about reasonable explanations for the other person's behavior. Even such statements as, "That doesn't sound like Jim; I wonder what is going on?" will help your colleague or customer shift gears back to rational problem-solving.

- Explore. Brainstorm next steps. Is it data collection, a meeting, a phone call, a trip to the other person's office? What makes sense?

Anna Maravelas says that she used this technique successfully hundreds of times. It has become second nature and is very effective.

Doug Thorburn, EA, CFP, has authored four books on alcohol and other drug addictions, including *Alcoholism Myths and*

Realities: Removing the Stigma of Society's Most Destructive Disease and *How to Spot Hidden Alcoholism: Using Behavioral Clues to Recognize Addiction in Its Early Stages.* The books have been endorsed by Congressman Jim Ramstad, *Skeptic Magazine* publisher Michael Shermer, and fellow addiction authors Claudia Black, Katherine Ketcham and Terrence Gorski. Out of 43 reviews of Doug's books at amazon.com, 34 are five-star. He has the following comments:

"In the extreme case, those dealing with anger management issues are often driven by what may be hidden (or not so hidden) alcoholism. Most of those required to attend anger management classes are in fact alcoholics. The classes are treating only a symptom of the underlying disorder, which must be treated first if there is to be any improvement in behavior."

Karen Sherman is the author of *Marriage Magic! Find it, Keep it, Make it Last.* She is a psychologist in New York with a specialty in relationships and lifestyle issues. She's been interviewed by *Men's Health, Family Circle* and XM Radio.

Her tips:

Most emotional behavior is "wired in" and occurs automatically when we are triggered by something in the present that reminds us (unknowingly) of something from the past.

Once we become aware of our patterns (because you cannot change anything you are not aware of), you can start to rewire these connections in your brain and make new connections.

Being more aware of your thoughts and body information basically does this.

Through a process of visualization, new connections can be made to heal old feelings. Once they are addressed, people can respond to present-day situations as they are, as opposed to just reacting to them. By not reacting emotionally, we can look at our choices and be more practical in our decision-making.

Laurie Puhn, JD, is a Harvard-educated attorney and a communications and relationship expert. She is the president of Laurie Puhn Communications, a professional and personal development training firm, and best-selling author of *Instant Persuasion: How to Change Your Words to Change Your Life*. She is also the host of the popular blog "Rudeness Interrupted" and author of "The Golden Rules of Tech-etiquette," as featured in the *Chicago Tribune*. Hailed by the *News Tribune* as "the Ann Landers of the New Millennium," Laurie has been a guest on numerous television shows, including ABC's *20/20*, Fox News Channel's *The Big Story* and *Fox & Friends*, CNN's *Tips from the Top* and *Good Day New York*. Her communication advice has been featured in *Reader's Digest, OC Family, Woman's Day, Maxim, Redbook, The New York Times, Newsday* and the *Chicago Tribune*, among other publications.

She speaks, writes and teaches about how to separate the emotional response from the logical response. The basic reason why people blunder in this area is not that they cannot control their anger. It is that even if they decide to be logical and practical, most people lack the communications skills to say the right thing to get what they want. The book *Instant Persuasion* and her teachings give people the exact words to use to win the respect, appreciation and attention they deserve. Once we become empowered with persuasive words, we can respond with solutions, ideas and assertive statements that offer insight and direct a conversation toward agreement.

A Note to the Reader

I trust that you enjoyed reading this work.

The message is loud and clear. We can choose how to utilize time, how to change roles in our day-to-day lives, and how to manage our lives with the time given to us. Time gives us the tools to learn how to behave, how to treat one another, how to give, how to receive, and how to be more productive and feel less overwhelmed by stress. Indeed, it is up to us to manage time and appreciate the beauty of living.

We are all born with only the desire to receive. In the course of our lives, over time, we grow and learn how to give, but we should never overlook or put aside how important we are. Toward the end of our lives, as we grow old, we once again become receivers more than givers. Why? Simply because we no longer have the tools, the energy, the strength and the capability to give. We regress and become needful, as babies are. We can never be complete givers if we don't understand how to receive. It is quite a challenge, but it can be done.

Time and timing are important factors. There is a proper place and time for everything. We can be open-minded, think clearly and practice the wisdom we've learned from experience.

I wish you more time, and plenty of it. May you enjoy it, love it, be enthused about it and utilize it with passion, logic, creativity and love for others. May the bright light shine for you, too, so that you can always find your own fulfillment and joy.

Ana H. B. Weber

My poem to you!

A Love Affair with Time

I have been there again and again

Playing the game just like you!

Searching for the light in the puddle of darkness,
containing a glimpse of hope
pointing deeper and stronger

Finding a momentary satisfaction with an intimate aura
connecting Smiles
between the cold tears through the passages of loving ...

Time,

You were always here for real

I didn't have to wait for you,
nervously passing the hard rock pavement on a foreign street,
sipping my hot coffee with such effort
reaching my unspoken voice

I selected a game of hide and seek instead
The magical circle of time designed with such perfection
Consumed with the need, running without aim

OFTEN barefoot, GOING where?

Will I find the fulfillment with the light shining low?
As my heart was aching and asking for more?
Filling the void perhaps?

I shifted from youth to maturity

I've come to know you so ... turning pain into laughter
and the company of drums playing a fast tune

Clicking a breathing heart to surrender

Time and time over again,

I learned to stay in the affair

You will always be
Voices ticking away,
Clocks everywhere
A noble reminder of ... You

Never stop, you don't look back
A handle of yesterday,
There is no reverse
but moving forward in the pace of life

I hug you till it hurts, I kiss you without touching you,
I feel you without holding you,
and I love you beyond imagination

I welcome you with every step I take

You are my UNCONDITIONAL FRIEND

Free of charge, free of risk and free of breaks

Your energy continues to amaze me

So where was I?
Giving me all I knew I had to have
Understanding the space to fill
With my desire

Passion running through my being
Savoring the taste and breathing you in,
endlessly in motion

TIME!

What would I do without you, my friend?

NOTHING AT ALL!

Pick up the crumbs of yesterday?

I choose to love you with the wisdom I've learned
throughout our honey-sweet and so colorful journey
together …

Such an affair …

978-0-595-41300-3
0-595-41300-5

www.ingramcontent.com/pod-product-compliance
Lightning Source LLC
Chambersburg PA
CBHW051413280526
45785CB00003B/1060